X-PLANES 10

NORTHROP FLYING WINGS

Peter E. Davies

SERIES EDITOR TONY HOLMES

OSPREY
PUBLISHING

OSPREY PUBLISHING
Bloomsbury Publishing Plc
PO Box 883, Oxford, OX1 9PL, UK
1385 Broadway, 5th Floor, New York, NY 10018, USA
E-mail: info@ospreypublishing.com
www.ospreypublishing.com

OSPREY is a trademark of Osprey Publishing

First published in Great Britain in 2019

A catalog record for this book is available from the British Library.

ISBN: PB 9781472825070; eBook 9781472825087;
ePDF 9781472825186; XML 9781472825094

19 20 21 22 23   10 9 8 7 6 5 4 3 2

Edited by Tony Holmes
Artwork by Adam Tooby
Index by Sandra Shotter
Typeset by PDQ Digital Media Solutions, Bungay, UK
Printed and bound in India by Replika Press Private Ltd.

Osprey Publishing supports the Woodland Trust, the UK's leading woodland
conservation charity.

To find out more about our authors and books visit www.ospreypublishing.com.
Here you will find extracts, author interviews, details of forthcoming events and
the option to sign up for our newsletter.

Front Cover
The second example of Northrop's
revolutionary XB-35 prototype bomber
(42-38323) made its first flight on
June 26, 1947, a year after 42-13603
had flown. The company's test crew
on both flights included Max R.
Stanley (pilot), Fred C. Brechter
(co-pilot), and Orval H. Douglas (flight
engineer). Although the aircraft
seemed to be from the distant future,
Stanley was dressed in a
contemporary flying suit and wore a
World War II-style soft leather helmet.
Brechter sat in the glazed area to his
right and Douglas was inside the cabin
managing a complex array of dials
and controls.
The brief 44-minute flight from the
company's Hawthorne, California,
base took the Flying Wing over the
mountains to Muroc Lake (later
Edwards AFB) to begin tests that
revealed serious propeller and
gearbox problems in both aircraft. Gun
turret-equipped 42-38323 made only
three more flights that year prior to
being placed in long-term storage in
the fall of 1948 and returned to
Hawthorne in USAF ownership in
January 1949, ending its career after
only eight flights, totaling 12 hours.
The piston-engined XB-35 was
replaced by the jet-powered YB-49
based on the same airframe. (Cover
artwork by Adam Tooby)

X PLANES

CONTENTS

FLAPS, similar to the ones
- other side

"Bustle"

PUSHER PROPELLER

NACELLE

WING

CHAPTER ONE

FLYING WING FASCINATIO

Few aircraft designs can trace their origins back directly to the 15th century, but there are conceptual links between Northrop Grumman's B-2 Spirit bomber of 2018 and Leonardo da Vinci's 1485 sketch of a bird-like ornithopter. Both are all-wing designs with no substantial fuselage or tail, although the da Vinci concept's man-powered flapping wings were clearly impractical. The desire to emulate this bird-like simplicity motivated designers for centuries. Combining low drag, high lift, and minimal weight, the machine's internal space could be used efficiently for fuel, engines, and cargo. The missing ingredient was the bird's skill in managing maneuverability and stability – still a problem for designers of all-wing aircraft today.

Nevertheless, attempts to realize da Vinci's dream persisted, proliferating in the 19th Century with steam-powered, dart-like vehicles from James Butler and Edmund Edwards, credible-looking flying wing glider designs by Alphonse Pénaud and gliders from Sir George Cayley, Louis Mouillard, and Otto Lilienthal. Pénaud flew models of his propeller-driven Planophore, a far-sighted forerunner of the conventional monoplane format, in 1871, and five years later he and Paul Gauchot designed a large amphibious flying wing with two tractor propellers. Its elliptical wing was covered in silk, and stability was to be provided by horizontal rudders in the flexible trailing edge. The pilot, in a small boat-shaped cockpit below the wing, had a glass canopy, and there was a retractable undercarriage. Pénaud was unable to secure funding to build it and, in despair, he committed suicide in 1880.

The Dunne D 8 swept-wing biplane, originally built in 1912 as the D 5, had a 60hp four-cylinder Green engine. John Dunne's biplane was the first in a series of successful tailless aircraft that enabled their inventor to develop ideas about stability, which were later studied by Jack Northrop. Licence-built and developed in the USA by Starling Burgess, the Dunne biplanes and seaplanes were tested by the US Army (as seen here in 1917) and the US Navy and were the first aircraft used by the Canadian Aviation Corps. (US Army Air Corps)

The first powered "birds" were facilitated by the advent of the internal combustion engine, enabling René Arnoux to build straight-winged craft with either pusher or puller two-blade propellers in 1913 and John Dunne to produce several swept-wing powered, tailless biplanes in 1911. During and immediately after World War I considerable advances occurred, particularly in Germany, although in the Soviet Union Boris Cheranovsky worked on tailless projects in the 1920s and Oleg Antonov in Ukraine produced his OKA-33 "motor glider" in 1937. In France, Charles Fauvel built his AV.2 powered flying wing in 1933.

Early designs by former heating appliance designer Hugo Junkers included the Nurflügel and JG 1 flying wings, both of which retained conventional tails. Originating in 1910, his JG 1 pioneered all-metal construction and was intended to carry passengers, although the Armistice restrictions on German aircraft manufacturing post-World War I forced Junkers to abandon the design. Undaunted, he continued to explore the flying wing's potential until his company was commandeered by the Nazis in 1935. His airliner designs included a much larger, 1,000-passenger J.1000 and the blended-wing, four-engine G.38 in 1927. Although the latter retained a conventional fuselage and tail, the thick aerofoil of its 144ft span wing allowed passengers to be carried in forward-facing cabins – an idea that Jack Northrop would develop in the 1940s.

Two other German designers responded to World War II's demand for new technologies. Reimar and Walter Horten, assisted (until his death in a Heinkel He 111 over Dunkirk) by another brother, Wolfram, designed numerous gliders in the 1930s. Their first tailless creation, the Ho 1 in 1933, was followed by the powered Ho 2 in 1934, which was flight-tested by the legendary Hanna Reitsch.

The Horten brothers were strongly influenced by fellow German, Alexander Lippisch, who had witnessed a flying demonstration near Berlin by Orville Wright in 1909. Lippisch had flown in World War I and later became an employee of the Zeppelin company and then Dornier, where he completed his first design, the Espenlaub E 2, in 1921. Lippisch's Delta IV and V both introduced and gave a name to the delta-wing aircraft. He continued to innovate after joining Messerschmitt in 1939, with proposals that led to the rocket-powered

Alexander Lippisch's Delta V was developed into the DFS 40 in 1937 and flown in 1939 by test pilot Heini Dittmar. Spanning 39ft 4in., it had a 100hp Argus pusher engine, rather than the 75hp tractor radial engine of its predecessor, the DFS 39 Delta IV. It crashed in a flat spin after launching with an incorrect center of gravity (cg) balance. (Nuricom1/Public domain)

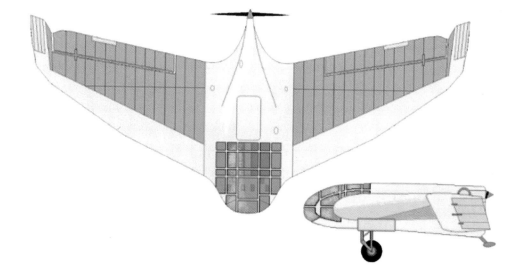

Me 163 fighter in 1940. It was based on the DFS 194 tailless glider, which Lippisch had evolved while working for Germany's Research Institute for Soaring Flight. After World War II, he was taken to the USA and assisted with the design of Convair's delta aircraft, specifically the XF-92, F-102 and F-106 fighters, and the B-58A supersonic bomber.

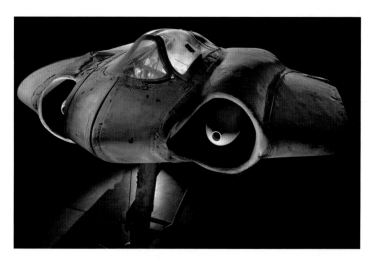

World War II gave the Horten brothers, as Luftwaffe officers with connections to Air Minister Generaloberst Ernst Udet, more opportunities to advance their projects. A fighter pilot from 1936, Walter had been wingman for high-scoring ace Major Adolf Galland on numerous occasions while flying Bf 109Es with *Jagdgeschwader* (JG) 26 during the Battle of Britain in 1940. Horten claimed seven RAF fighters destroyed (of which five were confirmed) during the campaign, and remained with JG 26 until May 1941, when he joined the flight staff of the RLM (*Reichsluftfahrtministerium* – Ministry of Aviation).

During his lengthy spell with the RLM, Horten flight-tested a captured Spitfire, which impressed him so much that he was convinced the Luftwaffe needed a far better fighter, preferably with a jet engine and a flying wing planform. When he became Inspector of Fighters, Horten encouraged work on a tailless version of the Me 262 fighter, as well as jet propulsion. He also met Lippisch and discussed the Me 163 at Peenemünde.

The Horten brothers' interest in flying wings was increased when they became aware of Jack Northrop's American XB-35 through an *Interavia* magazine feature, and they may well have seen his patent application for the flying wing aircraft in 1940, which would have been available to the public. Northrop's N-1M experimental flying wing was also given US news coverage in December 1941. The Hortens used these revelations to raise support for their own projects in Germany. Their early designs, like Northrop's, were powered versions of the gliders that Germany was allowed to build at the time, and although their Ho 7 resembled the N-9M, all these designers were working individually, but on similar ideas.

In 1943 the Hortens were given a research center at Göttingen airfield and construction facilities at Minden to design and produce the Ho IX fighter-bomber, which was to be fitted with two BMW 003 (later, Jumo 004) jet engines. It drew, to some extent, upon their 1938 crescent-wing Parabola as a true flying wing. Preceded by an unpowered glider version, designated the Ho IX V1, which was test-flown in March 1944, the powered V2 was flown in February 1945 at speeds up to 460mph. Although the Ho IX V1 was intended to eventually reach 720mph, it was destroyed in a crash-landing after two weeks' testing.

The Horten Ho IX V3 (Gotha Go 229) in storage within the Smithsonian National Air and Space Museum's Mary Baker Engen Restoration Hangar – its wooden wings are also kept here. One of the Go 229's highly innovative characteristics, perhaps unintentionally, was its low visibility to radar due to its shape and bonded-wood skin, making it one of the first "stealth" warplanes. Crucially, it also minimized "parasitic" drag (caused by external parts of an aircraft that do not provide lift), although its large air intakes created drag. A full-sized replica built by Northrop-Grumman in 2008 had its radar signature tested, and it was found to reflect about 40 percent of the radar energy of a single-engined World War II fighter when period radar detectors were employed. (Smithsonian National Air and Space Museum. NASM A-47513)

This archive photograph of the Ho 229 V3 in the USA shows the aircraft with its outer wing panels removed and undercarriage extended. (Photo by Eric Long, Smithsonian National Air and Space Museum. NASM 2000-9339)

Re-named the Gotha Go 229A shortly thereafter, the aircraft was ordered into production with an ejection seat, retractable undercarriage, four 30mm guns, and ordnance hard-points. However, its Friedrichsroda factory was captured by the Allies before any production examples had been completed. Several half-assembled Go 229s, including a nightfighter version and a two-seat attack bomber, were captured by the Allies. The almost-completed Go 229 V3 prototype was taken to Farnborough, Hampshire, in England, for evaluation, before being shipped on to the USA for analysis. Here, Jack Northrop examined both it and other Horten designs. Other partly completed examples were destroyed to prevent seizure by the Russians.

In the final 18 months of the war, the Hortens continued to work on a more advanced single-engined Ho X, supersonic Ho XIIIB (resembling Lippisch's DM 1) and a six-engined, 185ft span Horten XVIII *Amerika* bomber – a flying wing with which Hitler wanted to make a nuclear attack on New York. The flying wing, with six turbojet or turboprop engines, bore a passing resemblance to Northrop's 1946 XB-35 and even to the B-2A Spirit, ordered in 1981.

Postwar, Reimar Horten worked on flying wing designs in Argentina, including a Rolls-Royce Derwent-powered project and the DINFIA IA 38 flying wing transport aircraft (based on the Ho VIII), which flew in 1960. The Horten designs were undoubtedly a strong influence on similar concepts in America and Britain, apparently facilitated by the presence of a US spy working for the brothers in Argentina.

Other late wartime German flying wing studies included several with which Hitler hoped to fend off the increasing Allied air assault. Arado's Ar E.555-1 long-range bomber proposal in 1944 boasted six BMW 003A jet engines and remote-controlled gun turrets. It spawned fighter-sized jet derivatives with modified delta wings, but all were eventually canceled. The promising Blohm & Voss BV P 215 "emergency" nightfighter, several all-wing fighter and bomber designs from

Focke-Wulf and Heinkel, and a series of tailless bombers by Messerschmitt were also planned. Several of their designers, including Arado's Richard Vogt, and much of the research data moved to the USA after the war.

In Britain, John Dunne's tailless projects had led to Geoffrey Hill's Pterodactyl series of flying wings in 1924, developed with Westland Aircraft into a fighter for Air Ministry Specification F.3/32 in 1933. With endplate fins, a small lower wing (making it technically a sesquiplane),

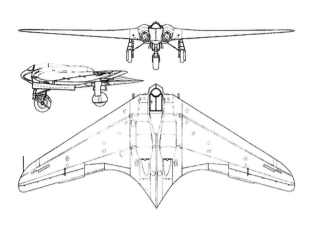

Spanning 55ft, the Go 229 V3 would have carried two 30mm cannon internally and two 2,204lb bombs on racks under the fuselage. The similar Ho IX V1 first flew in February 1945, and although the aircraft was lost early in the test program, it appeared that the planned maximum speed of 607mph at high altitude and an 1,860-mile range with two drop tanks were feasible. (Public domain)

and a speed of 190mph, it exhibited acceptable stability, but failed to enter production. In 1939 Hill extended his ideas into 140ft-span, all-wing bomber designs with four or six "pusher" piston engines. They had four remote-control gun turrets on the leading and trailing edges, a pilot/navigator position behind windows in the leading edge, and other features that coincided with aspects of Northrop's XB-35. A passenger version was also sketched, as was one that could carry its own fighter protection above its wing.

Other British designs in the 1930s originated from sailplanes, including the all-wing Baynes Bat towed glider, the 1939 Handley Page HP.75 Manx with twin pusher engines and small vertical fins, and the General Aircraft Ltd series of experimental gliders built between 1944 and 1948. Handley Page returned to the all-wing format in 1959 with the HP.117, a proposed 200-seat transport with up to six turbofans and boundary layer reduction to reduce drag.

Better known were the Armstrong Whitworth flying wings, which were steps towards a jet bomber. Studies leading to the A.W.50 began in 1942 and later incorporated four Metrovick turbojets and a tail-gun turret. The project evolved through the 112ft wingspan A.W.52G glider in 1945 to the A.W.52 jet with two Rolls-Royce Nenes and an ejection seat – the latter proved to be the first such British seat to be used in action when the prototype crashed. Tested between 1947 and 1953, the A.W.52 led to the A.W.56 bomber project with a more conventional fuselage (to hold a 10,000lb nuclear weapon) and a vertical tail. It incorporated boundary-layer control and laminar flow for improved transonic control in the attempt to reach a 500mph cruise speed with five Rolls-Royce Avon engines. Designed for the 1947 Operational Requirement 229, the A.W.56 eventually lost out to the early V-bomber proposals.

A more famous British tailless flying wing was the de Havilland DH 108. Despite encountering severe control and stability problems on many flights, John Derry managed to set a world speed record of 605.23mph in the third example in September 1948, thus becoming the first British pilot to achieve supersonic speed with the jet.

Further flying wing initiatives in Britain included Westland's P.J.D.144 twin-jet competitor to the DH 110 (Sea Vixen) and

Although they were only two years apart in serial number allocations, there was a world of difference between B-17G-70-DL Flying Fortress 44-6935 and the first XB-35 with the earlier serial 42-13603. Seen in May 1948, the Flying Wing has revised single-rotation, four-bladed propellers that were first flown on February 12, 1948 in an effort to reduce the vibration that plagued the original eight-bladed contra-rotating installation. The split flap wingtip rudders that became effective at 75mph were also used as airbrakes. (USAF)

the somewhat similar Hawker-Siddeley P.1077, although both included partial fuselages and twin vertical fins. Wilder drawing-board concepts encompassed Rolls-Royce's vertical take-off flying wing with up to 30 lift engines and four to provide forward propulsion – an early stage on the route to the Harrier. Perhaps the most spectacular was the Vickers Swallow. The latter, originating in 1946, used Sir Barnes Wallace's ideas of combining a swing-wing with a tailless design to produce a supersonic nuclear bomber. Four swiveling jet engines were mounted near the wingtips, and missile-armed fighter versions were conjectured as well as further strike and transport derivatives using the same concept.

In the USA during the same period, there was also interest in flying wing or tailless designs. Boeing developed its prototype XB-15 long-range bomber, predecessor to the smaller B-17, into a tailless Model 306 bomber proposal with four piston engines and a 140ft wing, with elevons extending rearwards on booms attached to the trailing edges. Around 1941, Consolidated Aircraft drew out a flying wing alternative to its B-36 intercontinental bomber proposal with a massive 288ft wingspan and six 3,000hp radial engines to carry a 10,000lb bomb-load to Germany from the USA and 72,000lbs over shorter distances. North of the border, the Canadian Car and Foundry Company submitted a flying wing proposal for the same specification that generated the XB-36 and Northrop's XB-35. Designed by Vincent Burnelli, a Texan with a pioneering interest in all-wing and lifting body designs, the B-2000B had a twin-boom tail that relied on a blended wing and fuselage aerodynamic shape.

However, the only serious contender for practical flying wing initiatives in the USA was former California garage mechanic John Knudsen Northrop, who had no training in aeronautical engineering. In his youth he had studied the flight of seabirds, made paper and balsa-wood model gliders to try and emulate it and endured the scepticism of his friends when he proposed building aircraft with the same characteristics. He reasoned that the only really essential part of an aircraft was the wing. A fuselage served mainly to support a stabilizing tail unit, and it could be incorporated in the wing. By 1939 he was ready to realize his ambition.

CHAPTER TWO

THE NORTHROP SOLUTION

Born in Newark, New Jersey, in 1895, Jack Northrop grew up in Santa Barbara, California. America's aircraft companies were beginning to form in that area, and aged 16, he saw a French pilot assemble and fly a home-made aircraft on a Santa Barbara lawn and decided that he could do better himself. Commenting on his entry into the aviation design business, he recalled with typical modesty that he had a little experience as a garage mechanic while at school, a year working as an assistant architectural draughtsman and part-time work for his father's carpentry and building business, and that this "somehow qualified me to design airplanes." In fact, his skills in mathematics and draughtsmanship without a college degree were impressive at an early age, and he had spent many hours sketching his own ideas for airplanes.

Hearing of an aircraft-building project by Allan and Malcolm Loughead (later, "Lockheed") in the premises next to the State Street, Santa Barbara, garage where he worked, Northrop often visited them. He offered to provide proper engineering drawings and stress computations to help with their trial-and-error methods of construction for their first aircraft, before joining them as a draughtsman. In his designs he focused on strength and simplicity at a time when aircraft were fragile wood and wire structures. Northrop worked on the early Loughead F-1 74ft span seaplane of 1916, which won the brothers considerable acclaim.

That same year, with the Lougheads' Aircraft Manufacturing Company and former stunt pilot Anthony Stadlman, he designed the graceful S-1 Sport biplane that featured a moulded monocoque fuselage inspired by a captured German Albatros D Va. Although

Northrop's N-1M on an early test flight in 1940 with down-turned wingtips and the windshield located further from the leading edge. The Lycoming 0-146 engines were soon replaced with 117hp Franklin 6AC264F2s and three-bladed propellers, which were just about powerful enough to take the N-1M to 4,000ft. It made around 55 flights until mid-1941, with the wing at various leading-edge sweep and wing dihedral angles and the preferred level wingtip option, but always with overheating engines that still lacked power. (Terry Panopalis collection)

The Loughead S-1 Sport biplane, a "sportsman's airplane for use in pleasure and business," had a smooth, laminated fuselage, minimal rigging, and folding wings for storage and transport. Its lower wing was highly innovative, for it could rotate to act as an airbrake or landing flap for landings at 30mph. Its high price compared with the cheap army surplus aircraft then available during a slump in aviation sales destroyed its commercial potential, but gave Northrop the technology to design the successful Lockheed Vega monoplane. (San Diego Air and Space Museum/ Public domain)

neither the F-1 or the S-1 entered production, Allan Loughead secured US Navy contracts to build two Curtiss HS-2L flying boats, on which Northrop also worked after being drafted into the US Army but reassigned to Loughead in view of his aviation skills. The company was forced to close in 1920, however, after the HS-2Ls had been completed.

Jack then spent three years working in his father's building firm before finding employment with Donald Douglas' aircraft company in Santa Monica, California, from 1923 to 1926. His tasks included wing-building for the one-off Cloudster, which was designed to make the first non-stop coast-to-coast flight across the USA. He also contributed to the wing design of Charles Lindbergh's Ryan M-1 monoplane *Spirit of St Louis* in 1926, improving the aircraft's range through structural streamlining of the wing and the removal of bracing. By 1926 Northrop had incorporated his fuselage structure for the S-1 Sport into a design proposed by Jerry Vultee that incorporated a clean, cantilever wing. He suggested it to Allan Lockheed, who raised finance for what became the very successful 200mph Vega monoplane of 1927. The 132 examples subsequently built put Lockheed back in business.

As he set out to establish his own series of companies, Northrop always believed that they should be "a good place to work," with a family atmosphere. He made a point of speaking to the workforce (which he christened his "Norcrafters") every week to keep them up to date on company developments, and he would often be found working alongside them. This, in turn, inspired great loyalty and belief in Northrop's vision, although, as his test pilot Jon Myers later judged, he was a "great genius" but lacked skill as a businessman, relying on others to try and finance his dreams.

Lacking support for his flying wing concepts during his time at Lockheed, Jack Northrop left in 1928 with accountant Ken Jay to pursue advanced ideas in all-metal construction and flying wings with their new company Avion Corporation. This enterprise was sponsored by George Hearst, a son of millionaire William Randolph Hearst. Northrop was replaced at Lockheed by Jerry Vultee, who developed the Vega monoplane into the larger Explorer, Wiley Post's Orion-Explorer and Charles Lindbergh's Sirius floatplane.

Avion's Model 1 ("The Wing") in 1929 developed the idea of clean, smooth airframes, uncluttered by rigging, biplane wings or other drag-creators. It was similar to a glider that Anthony Stadlman had designed in 1927 before he and Northrop parted company. The Model 1 had an innovative stressed-skin metal wing containing the open cockpits and 90hp Menasco Motors Pirate four-cylinder engine (built by one of Northrop's friends to replace a Cirrus Mk III) with a shaft-driven pusher propeller, later moved to the nose. The design, which retained a tail boom with fin and tailplane, was eventually called the Northrop Flying Wing. Northrop also worked on his Alpha all-metal, stressed-skin low-wing monoplane with multi-cellular construction that attracted the attention of William E. Boeing, whose company had been absorbed into United Aircraft as a way of surviving the 1929 economic depression.

This Detroit Aircraft Corporation-built DL-1B (a seven-seat variant of the Lockheed Vega transport) was evaluated by the USAAC as the Y1C-17 (31-408). It was lost on March 10, 1931 when a clogged fuel line caused a damaging forced landing after a 1,740-mile journey. Designed by Northrop and Gerald Vultee, Vegas made the first flight around the world (by Wiley Post) and over the North Pole, together with trans-oceanic flights by Amelia Earhart and many other record-breaking expeditions. (National Museum of the Air Force 081030-F1234S-007)

Northrop Aircraft Corporation also became a division of United Aircraft, being incorporated in January 1930 into a new facility at Burbank, California. However, lack of finance soon forced Northrop's company to amalgamate with Stearman and then, in 1932, with Douglas Aircraft at Inglewood, California, as a new Northrop-led El Segundo Division to concentrate on research and development. Jack Northrop was able to work with a young Ed Heinemann on wind-tunnel models of his tailless Model 25 and Project 9 – a twin-engined tailless bomber design with end-plate fins.

Ken Jay remained on board and Douglas designer Ed Heinemann joined him at Northrop. Flying wing projects were subsequently put on hold for ten years while Jack Northrop concentrated on more profitable conventional types for the USAAF such as the A-16 and A-17 monoplanes. The latter was the standard USAAF attack bomber in the late 1930s, developed from Northrop's Gamma two-seat, high-altitude monoplane, which had been the first aircraft to overfly the South Pole. In 1937 Douglas bought out Northrop and dissolved Jack's company, causing 1,400 redundancies.

Jack, frustrated by the lack of design opportunities, resigned on January 1, 1938. His third company, Northrop Aircraft, Inc. was established in March 1939 with the profits of the Douglas buy-out. The new, small organization in Hawthorne, California, was set up in a yellow-painted, black widow spider-ridden former hotel/brothel for oil workers. Northrop gathered a team of top engineers, as well as test pilots Edward Bellande and Moye Stephens, and La Motte T. Cohu, a TWA director who became their forceful general manager. A far-sighted businessman who was aware of the imminence of war, Cohu was anxious to create new manufacturing facilities.

Yellow became the color for all Northrop test aircraft and the name "Black Widow" would be chosen by the company for its successful P-61 nightfighter of 1941. A 72-acre production site for more than 100 employees was ready by 1940. Northrop, a quiet, shy man who focused on his engineering, also developed a reputation as a modest, caring employer who inspired his team, while Cohu encouraged him to look beyond research and seek production contracts within a deteriorating world political situation. Capital came in via accountant Ted Coleman, and their first company-financed research project, the N-1M (a "flying mock-up," hence the "M" in the designation) became Northrop's first, long-desired proof-of-concept flying wing.

The N-1M's true flying wing configuration is evident in this view. The pusher position for the Franklin engines was carried over into the XB-35 design, but with long drive shafts from "buried" engines. The "cap" over the windscreen gave a little more headroom for the pilot. The lighter areas of wing inboard of the registration are cover strips for the joints where the wing dihedral, twist and sweepback could be adjusted. Pilot Moye Stephens is just visible in the cockpit. (Terry Panopalis collection)

Walt Cerny headed the designers, working closely with aerodynamicist Herb DeCenzo. Ed Zap (who invented split flaps) and the eminent Dr Theodore von Kármán, Director of the Daniel Guggenheim School of Aeronautics at the California Institute of Technology and a supporter of flying wings, became consultants. In 1941, von Kármán was joined by his assistant at "Cal Tech," Dr William Sears, and the work undertaken by both men would prove to be critically important when it came to turning the flying wing design into a practical proposition.

The all-wing concept was still mainly theoretical at this point, and Northrop's team faced many challenges in ensuring stability and spin-free flight. Inspiration came from unlikely sources, including a Zanonia macrocarpa seed, sent from Australia, which had a curved flying wing shape about five inches across and a seed in its "nose." It could glide with stability and spin-resistance – the seed had already inspired Czech designer Igo Etrich to build a Zanonia-shaped aircraft as early as 1909.

Von Kármán gave Northrop his calculations on wing loading with different angles of attack (AoA) and aspect ratios, supported later by test models in the Cal Tech wind tunnel. Northrop had already worked out that an all-wing design could reduce drag by 40 percent and save a tenth of overall weight compared with conventional layouts, thereby increasing range by 20 percent.

He also realized that different methods of flying control would be needed in the absence of a tail. As he noted, "Rudders for all-wing aircraft are perhaps the chief control difficulty. Unless large fins are used, a conventional rudder cannot be employed." Instead, Northrop introduced pure drag rudders, realizing that "a double split trailing-edge flap at the wingtip has been found to have the most satisfactory all-round characteristics." The split flaps performed the role of trim tabs too.

It was also clear that the side forces acting on aircraft with tail fins were absent in all-wing designs, denying the pilot the "cross-wing force [that] is probably important for precision flight such as tight formation flying, bombing runs, gun training maneuvers or pursuit. This importance arises because with low side-force it becomes difficult to judge when side-slip is taking place as the angle of bank necessary to sustain a steady side-slipping motion is small." These characteristics would later be criticized in Northrop's XB-49 when it was evaluated as a bombing platform, and they could only be alleviated by auto-stabilization devices, which were still in their infancy.

To finance a flying wing project, the company took on wartime defense work, producing airframe parts for B-17s and PBY Catalinas. It also received contracts for its first in-house commercial design, the

N-3PB Nomad floatplane, and began studies for the XP-56 tailless fighter. Delivery of the first of 24 N-3PBs to its sole customer, the Royal Norwegian Navy Air Service in exile in Canada, commenced in December 1940, just eight months after initiating the design process. At the time it was the fastest floatplane in service, reaching 256mph despite its two large Edo floats.

Northrop almost became the second source for the Douglas SBD-3 Dauntless dive-bomber for the US Navy – an aircraft that Jack Northrop had partially designed while with Douglas. The decision was reversed when Donald Douglas discovered that many of the Northrop workers had left jobs at Douglas, including Dauntless production, to join Jack. Furious, Northrop rejected a profitable compensatory offer to be a sub-contractor on the project. Instead, he did agree to a 200-unit contract to produce Vultee A-31-NO Vengeance dive-bombers for the RAF. The aircraft failed to impress Northrop as a design, but it gave the company a profitable base for its flying wing research.

Moye Stephens occupies the N-1M's cockpit while Jack Northrop poses for publicity shots on December 4, 1941. A flight demonstration for the Press followed shortly afterwards. (Terry Panopalis collection)

In the days before computer modeling, Northrop's feasibility tests were done with paper or balsa models, with flight tests in the local dance hall and the National Advisory Committee for Aeronautics (NACA) spin tunnel, which demonstrated that the full-size 38ft-span N-1M was very unlikely to spin. However, there were specific problems with stability, particularly while turning, in lack of symmetry if an engine failed and with center of gravity (cg) as fuel burned off. Dr Sears' assistant, Irv Ashkenas, worked on the design for the flying controls and was responsible for the innovative control systems in Northrop's later flying wings, including the first fully powered hydraulic controls used in the N-9M.

Northrop was aware that earlier designs by Lippisch and Hill in Europe had suffered from poor directional stability, so he incorporated (at von Kármán's suggestion) drooped wingtips, constructed so that they could be modified to a straight configuration. When drooped they would act partially as rudders, but the main controls were Horten-style combined ailerons and elevators, or "elevons," together with split clamshell drag rudders doubling as speed-brakes in the wingtips or to trim out a lost engine situation. The elevons acted independently like ailerons for banking when the control column was moved left or right, and together to provide pitch control like elevators when the column moved fore and aft. Drooped wingtips were found to have no real advantage for directional stability (although they would be re-introduced for Northrop's later XP-56) and they actually reduced lift.

The N-1M used mahogany and spruce, with metal where it was essential. Power came from two "buried" 65hp Lycoming O-145 four-cylinder engines with two-bladed pusher propellers on ten-foot drive shafts. Construction was completed by the end of June 1940 and the aircraft was taken to Baker Dry Lake for its first flight by contract test pilot Vance Breese (who later made the first P-51 Mustang flight) on July 3. Initial taxi trials revealed that the all-yellow "Jeep" (the aircraft received the nickname after the yellow, magical "Eugene the Jeep" in *Popeye* comics) had cg problems that made it unable to rotate. The N-1M climbed briefly above ten feet, but only when the undercarriage hit a bump.

The nose-wheel strut was lengthened when it was found that the aircraft was 200lbs overweight and needed a steeper AoA for take-off. This in turn necessitated the fitting of a tailwheel "bumper" on a stub ventral fin to prevent propeller damage at a steep ground angle. However, it was clear that the machine could not perform any better with its underpowered engines. The aircraft required constant back-pressure on the control column and the use of a trailing edge trim-flap to adjust its height effectively up to a ten-foot maximum altitude.

Moye Stephens (company secretary and sole test pilot) took over the test-flights, and on one occasion a propeller was knocked off and a rear spar was fractured. The elevons were extended rearwards because the airflow was separating over the thick wing, rendering them ineffective at high AoA. This added another five feet of altitude. To save time on the frequent return journeys to Hawthorne for modifications, the N-1M was towed like a glider to Muroc behind a C-47. Northrop reported that pilots found that it was "absolutely normal in every respect. It feels and flies just like any other airplane. Any competent pilot could fly it with no difficulty."

FLYING BOTTLE

The N-2B/XP-56 Black Bullet was designed in response to a February 1940 requirement for a single-engined fighter capable of reaching up to 525mph at 15,000ft and able to match contemporary European fighters in overall performance. The US Army Air Corps' (USAAC) R-40C competition that stemmed from this requirement encouraged some highly innovative responses, including the Vultee XP-54 "Swoose" with twin tail-booms, and the Curtiss-Wright XP-55 Ascender with a pusher engine and canard elevator.

Northrop's submission was tailless, with a 42.5ft span, a chubby 23.5ft fuselage or "crew nacelle" and heavy armament concentrated in the nose. It was the first all-magnesium aircraft, made with Northrop's new Heliarc arc-welding process devised by Tom Piper and Vladimir Pavlecka, who was responsible

The N-1M in October 1943 after repainting, but before the application of USAAF insignia for display purposes and storage at Freeman Field, Indiana. The tiny aircraft proved the flying wing concept to Northrop's satisfaction, and within two years he was planning to use it to satisfy the USAAF's ambitious 1941 MX-140 requirement for a bomber that could carry a 10,000lb bomb-load more than 10,000 miles at 300mph with a service ceiling of 40,000ft. (Terry Panopalis collection)

for much of the XP-56 design. Magnesium, welded in a helium atmosphere so that it did not ignite, was used as it was lighter and more readily available than aluminum, although it was more inflammable and had to be welded rather than riveted to prevent bi-metallic corrosion.

The XP-56 was the first aircraft to have "pusher" contra-rotating propellers, and it also introduced the idea of an air-cooled engine (an R-2800-29 Double Wasp rather than the preferred, but canceled, Pratt & Whitney H-2600 liquid-cooled option) fully buried in the fuselage and driving Curtiss Electric contra-rotating propellers. This installation, which required a fuselage re-design to take the larger R-2800, was a notorious source of penetrating noise. If a pilot needed to bail out, the propeller and gearbox assembly could be jettisoned with a detonating cord. Although it had vertical fins above and below the tail and down-turned wingtips like the N-1M, its stability problems were evident.

After five months of delays, mainly due to the change in powerplant, the first aircraft (42-1786) flew twice on September 6, 1943 at Muroc in silver finish with a yellow spinner. After modifications to the dorsal fin, it flew again on October 8, but tumbled out of control when the left main gear tyre exploded during a high-speed landing run, possibly due to broken glass on the runway. It flipped over several times and came to rest inverted in a dust cloud, injuring test pilot John Myers' back and ankle when he and his seat were thrown out through the canopy. Fortunately, he had chosen to wear a reinforced polo helmet rather than the usual soft "hat."

The second prototype (XP-56A 42-38353, with increased wingspan, enlarged dorsal fin, and stronger tyres) could not reach its design speed of 467mph after seven flights and still showed low-speed lateral instability, tail-heaviness, and control reversal. Wind-tunnel tests were planned to try and improve its stability, but after long delays and the increasing availability of jet fighters, the XP-56A was stored following its final flight on August 11, 1944 and eventually donated to the Smithsonian Institution.

The first XP-56 was originally painted in three-tone British camouflage paint, but it was re-finished in silver for its first flight on September 6, 1943. The aircraft's token vertical stabiliser brought it closer to Northrop's flying wing ideal, although the bullet-shaped fuselage and dorsal fin were more conventional features. (National Museum of the Air Force 061024-F-1234P-009)

The N-2B/XP-56 Black Bullet was designed by Northrop in response to a February 1940 requirement for a single-engined fighter capable of reaching up to 525mph at 15,000ft. The first aircraft to have "pusher" contra-rotating propellers, it also introduced the idea of an air-cooled engine fully buried in the fuselage and driving Curtiss Electric contra-rotating propellers. (National Museum of the Air Force 061024-F-1234P-008)

AMERICA'S FIRST ROCKET PLANE

Northrop's next fighter project, in 1942, reverted to the all-wing format and benefited from von Kármán's expertise, through the Aerojet Engineering Corporation

NORTHROP XP-56

The second XP-56 is depicted here in standard USAAF camouflage and markings in March 1944. After a landing accident with the first example, the cg was moved forwards on the second aircraft and the ventral fin had a small wheel fitted to prevent it from digging into the ground. It also had slightly longer wingtips for the ram-air intakes. Instability problems and lack of useable power prevented the XP-56 from reaching its intended 467mph top speed and 33,000ft service ceiling.

(of which von Kármán was currently president), in rocket propulsion to devise a craft that reflected German progress with the rocket-powered He 176 and Me 163. The MX-324 and its preceding MX-334 glider configuration were full-size mock-ups for the XP-79 rocket-powered fighter. A prone pilot position had to be used to increase his resistance to g-forces and enable a thinner central wing profile. The pilot had to pull himself into the cockpit on his belly, using the upper escape hatch to enter the tiny space.

Most of the development tasks went to the Air Materiel Center (AMC) at Wright Field, under Northrop supervision, since the company was already overburdened with production work on a series of conventional monoplanes for military contracts. The wooden-winged structure was stressed to 18g, used a skid landing gear like the Me 163 (later replaced by three fixed-wheel units) and had a small vertical fin attached, although Northrop hoped that would be temporary.

Three were built and flight-tested, tow-launched initially by a powerful Cadillac car and later air-towed by a P-38 fighter. This led to the loss of the one example when it was caught in the propeller wash of the P-38 after release and spiraled down inverted, out of control. Pilot Harry Crosby managed to extricate himself and sit on the underside of the inverted glider as it slowly descended, before finally sliding off to parachute down. He was pursued in his descent by the glider, which continued to circle around him upside down. Test pilot Alex Papana also accidentally pulled the lever to jettison both upper and lower cockpit hatches instead of using the adjacent lever to release the tow-line from the P-38, although he made a safe landing.

In June 1944 the second example was fitted with an Aerojet-General 2,000lb thrust rocket motor as the MX-324 "Rocket Wing," with aniline and oxidizer tanks either side of the pilot and neoprene curtains to protect him from leakage of the lethal propellants. Its elevons also acted as airbrakes. On July 5, 1944 Harry Crosby cast his MX-324 adrift from the P-38 and fired up the 200lb thrust Aerojet XCAL-200 to make the first flight by an American rocket-powered aircraft. Several more flights were made, eventually reaching 350mph in a dive, although the shortcomings of the rocket limited the program's usefulness, so both surviving aircraft were withdrawn a month later.

FLYING RAM

The XP-79 fighter, subject of a January 12, 1943 USAAF contract, was designed in two versions, namely the NS-14 with one Aerojet-General 2,000lb thrust rocket motor assisted by booster rockets on take-off and the NS-14B (MX-365, or XP-79B) with two 1,600lb thrust Westinghouse 19B (J30) turbojets. The rocket plane, at 13,500lbs all-up weight, would have been about 5,000lbs heavier than the NS-14B. They were intended to reach speeds up to 545mph, and the jet version's maximum range of 993 miles was more than twice that of the NS-14A.

The rocket's highly volatile fuming nitric acid oxidizer had caused several terrible accidents in other rocket aircraft such as the Me 163, and the all-magnesium structure had to be reinforced with steel plates in places to protect the fuel tanks from bullets. It was later claimed that the steel-reinforced wing leading edge of the XP-79B version was intended to cut into enemy aircraft in ram attacks, and this became a widely accepted view that was even supported by Jack Northrop. Others involved in the project dismissed the idea as an AMC publicity man's gimmick in origin, pointing out the suicidal probabilities of such an attack. Any operational developments of the design were, in any case, intended to carry four forward-firing 0.50-cal machine guns outboard of the air intakes. A four-skid retractable undercarriage was initially used, with a catapult or wheeled dolly for launching.

Work on the XP-79 was subcontracted to a local company, coincidentally called Avion, Inc., due to pressure of work on wartime contracts for Northrop's radar-equipped N-8 (P-61 Black Widow) nightfighter and the Vengeance dive-bomber. An XP-79B version was devised in mid-1943 with a second Westinghouse 19-B engine in place of the rocket motor, but the rocket-powered XP-79 was canceled in September 1944 when it was clear that there were intractable problems with the Aerojet motor. Avion also added one, then two vertical stabilizers as it doubted Northrop's claims regarding stability. The estimated performance of both variants was similar, peaking at 547mph at sea level.

By September 1944 it was clear that the small Avion Company was having difficulty completing the aircraft and handling the complex magnesium construction processes, so work was moved back to

Harry Crosby adopted a prone position in the MX-334 glider, with twin tow-lines attached to a P-38 Lightning. The rudderless vertical stabilizer had six bracing wires and aerodynamic "boots" surrounded the landing gear. (USAAF)

Northrop's crowded facility. By June 1945 it had the XP-79B ready for high-speed taxi trials at Muroc after further delays with tyres and brakes, and the first flight took place on September 12, despite a fire truck crossing the pilot's path as he neared take-off speed. Jack Northrop reported that "for 15 minutes the airplane was flown in a beautiful demonstration. The pilot [air racer Harry Crosby] indicated mounting confidence by executing more and more maneuvers of a type that would not be expected unless he was thoroughly satisfied with the behavior of the airplane. After about 15 minutes the airplane entered what appeared to be a normal slow roll from which it did not recover. This accident to the only completed XP-79 brought an end to the program."

Crosby had attempted to bail out when the XP-79's nose dropped and it developed an uncontrollable roll, but he was struck by the aircraft and fell to his death.

FLYING BOMB

An unusual, pilotless offshoot of the smaller N-1M-type projects was the JB-1, a 2,000lb flying "buzz bomb" with a pair of 400lbs thrust General Electric B1 turbojets based on the company's turbo-superchargers for piston engines and an intended range of 200 miles. Early tests showed the inadequacy of the jet engines, resulting in Ford PJ-31-1 pulse jets (based on the Fieseler motor used in German V1 "doodlebugs") being selected for a slightly larger, re-designated version known as the JB-10. It had a Heliarc-welded magnesium airframe with a circular shroud covering the pulse-jet in a new, rounded fuselage and a 186-mile range.

Ten flights were made, using a sled powered by five Monsanto rockets to encourage the JB-10 "Jet Bomb" into the air, but ten of the eleven

NEXT PAGES

NORTHROP P-79B IN COMBAT

The prone-piloted XP-79B was intended to evolve into a machine gun-armed jet or rocket-powered interceptor. The loss of the only completed prototype and test pilot Harry Crosby on its first flight in September 1945 ended that prospect after only 15 minutes of flight time. With its two Westinghouse 19-B jet engines, a service version should have attained 547mph and a range of 993 miles at altitudes up to 40,000ft, potentially making it a useful interceptor or escort fighter if World War II had continued into 1946.

produced experienced various control failures, so the program was ended in January 1946. Jack Northrop reported that "in spite of its peculiar configuration, which departed appreciably from the all-wing ideal, it had quite good flight characteristics." One of these was that the JB-1 developed so much lift in ground effect that it was often very difficult to persuade it to land. The same characteristic was later noted in the XB-35 and YB-49, which tended to "float" at minimum approach speed, causing a potential overshoot. Like so many other concurrent designs, the JB-10 was let down by engines that never developed adequate, reliable performance, and by a series of control problems.

Although World War II had given Northrop the chance to flight-test many of his innovative projects experimentally, the company's relatively conventional Black Widow was its most successful contribution to that conflict. In financial terms, profits from manufacturing B-17 engine cowlings exceeded those from the 1,000-unit P-61 contract awarded to Northrop by the USAAF, and the company's relationship with Boeing was to have valuable long-term benefits.

An XP-79B prone pilot, lying in a very cramped cockpit that was stressed for 12g and peering out through the transparent nose area, controlled pitch and roll with a crossbar that had hand-grips at each end. He used foot pedals to operate the rudder/airbrakes, which in turn were powered by bellows controls driven by wingtip venturi air inlets that also appeared on the second XP-56. The pilot's head was supported by a large chin-rest. A quadricycle undercarriage replaced skids on the sole XP-79B from July 1943 to provide adequate stability. (National Museum of the Air Force 110516F-XN622-003ain)

Northrop's JB-1 ("Jet Bomb") was a direct derivative of the MX-324 "Rocket Wing", with magnesium and aluminum construction and programmable automatic gyro/servo controls. The explosives were housed in two cylindrical shapes, faired into the wing center-section. A piloted glider version was also built to prove the basic concept. (San Diego Air and Space Museum/Public domain)

CHAPTER THREE

BIG WING – B-35

Northrop's original large flying wing proposal emphasized the cost-saving possibilities of a one-piece unit without extra fuselage and tail structures. It also advocated the benefits of even payload weight distribution, rather than having to reinforce one part of an airframe to carry bombs or cargo, and claimed a 20 percent increase in speed over a conventional aircraft with the same powerplants and payload. With the N-9M, the basis of that concept began to be realized. (Terry Panopalis collection)

Northrop's best hope of success with the flying wing concept arose out of fears that Britain would be overrun by Nazi Germany, thus requiring a fleet of massive transatlantic bombers to attack occupied Europe directly from US territory. This philosophy, based on the theory that "the bomber will always get through," was severely tested when the Eighth Air Force's daylight attacks on Germany began in 1942. It gave rise to Boeing's B-29 Superfortress, with a 3,000-mile range, in 1940 and its successor after competition with Boeing proposals, Convair's 200-ton, 230ft-span B-36 Peacemaker with a 10,000-mile range. The B-36's size, weight, and range required up to ten engines, vast quantities of fuel and heavy defensive armament due to its limited speed. As a mainly conventional design, its development time was expected to be fairly short.

From the outset, Jack Northrop felt that he could reach the required specification with a smaller, simpler aircraft. After meetings with AMC officers, he was invited to propose an alternative all-wing design, the XB-35, on the understanding that it would take longer to develop and could perhaps replace the B-36, thanks to its proposed ability to carry 10,000lbs of bombs on two-way Atlantic crossings.

Jack Northrop, in close contact with Gen Henry "Hap" Arnold, Chief of the USAAC, throughout this period, assured the latter that: "We can build transport or bomber aircraft of any size over 25,000lbs gross weight which will do the same job as a similar airplane of conventional design and have a high speed of 75 to 100mph greater. I think we can obtain the same high speeds as attained with conventional aircraft with, roughly, half the amount of power."

Much of this claim clearly relied on reduced drag, although Northrop also promoted "the simplicity of the straight line structure, the large amount of space available for the housing of retractable landing gears, fuel tanks, bomb-bays, etc., and the ease with which airplanes of this configuration can be armed." Test pilots' later verdicts on the N-9M test models for the XB-35 seemed to support his claims.

These attractive prospects generated much interest at Air Material Division, and although the Battle of Britain's success would ultimately enable existing US bombers to operate from England, the USAAC's interest in a flying wing bomber persisted. Northrop was invited in May 1941 to produce "design studies of a flying wing type of bomber." Project engineer Walt Cerny was told that it would need a range of 10,000 miles, a combat speed range between 240 and 450mph and a ceiling of 40,000ft. It would have heavy protective armor and a minimum defensive armament of six 37mm cannon and eight 0.50-cal machine guns. It was suggested to him that the bomber was a "first national priority." Northrop received a USAAC contract on October 30, 1941 to begin design work on Project MX-140 (the XB-35), including a mock-up and an N-9M single-seat simulator aircraft, with a delivery date of November 1943 for the first bomber. He was also offered an attractive joint deal on a flying wing troop and cargo carrier project by industrialist Henry J. Kaiser in 1942, but declined it for fear of delaying his bomber project. Meanwhile, Convair, which heard of the latter, sketched a 288ft span, six-engined flying wing bomber that was then shelved when the company received a letter of intent to order 100 B-36s in July 1943.

Tests in NACA's Ames Laboratory full-scale wind tunnel, Moffett Field facility and Langley Field spin tunnel indicated that the N-9M had acceptable stall and spin characteristics, but led to the installation of a fully powered hydraulic control system. In the N-9M's cramped cockpit, the seat and rudder pedals were not adjustable. When stalled, it tended to tumble around its pitch axis (an imaginary line drawn from wingtip to wingtip), although the wingtip slots improved this undesirable trait. (Terry Panopalis collection)

SCALE SIMULATOR

Inadequate engines had undermined several previous Northrop designs, and for the one-third scale N-9M only 260hp six-cylinder Menasco C6S-4 air-cooled engines were available, using a pair to simulate four twin-propeller engines planned for the XB-35. Spanning 60ft (roughly one third of the XB-35's eventual 172ft) and weighing 6,235lbs, the N-9M was an all-wing design that was to be ready to fly within 30 months. Its deadline was soon extended when work was suspended after the attack on Pearl Harbor, which forced Northrop to concentrate on its combat aircraft contracts.

The N-9M's structure was similar to the N-1M's, using mainly wood with some steel tubing and aluminum, but it included hydraulic-powered control systems intended for the XB-35. Its wing incorporated elevons, landing flaps, flaps to control pitch and

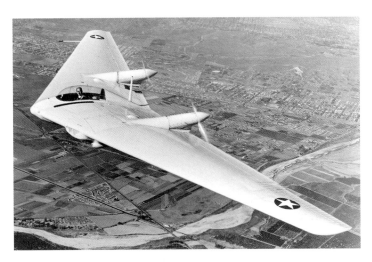

The first N-9M cruises over California with John Myers in charge. The N-9Ms were not issued military serial numbers as they were "engineering development tools" rather than aircraft, but as military projects they were not given civilian serial numbers either. (Terry Panopalis collection)

others on the wingtips, acting as rudders or airbrakes by creating drag at each tip. The first N-9M had forward-opening airbrakes (painted with shark's teeth and topically named "Japsnappers"), but they were never fully tested. Its single-seat cockpit, with a bubble canopy, allowed an observer to sit sideways behind the pilot if a fuel tank was removed. Jack Northrop made one flight in this uncomfortable position.

Two back-up N-9Ms (N-9M-2 and N-9MA) were requested in a follow-up contract on September 10, 1942 to supplement wind-tunnel tests, including many in the vertical spin tunnel that was used decades later to test models of the Northrop Grumman B-2 Spirit. While exploring the control challenges inherent in the flying wing concept, it was shown that the N-9M could roll, loop, and recover from stalls like other fighter-sized aircraft.

Chief test pilot John Myers began ground tests on December 20, 1942 and made the N-9M's first flight a week later, before handing over to Max Constant. Most flights yielded little research data due to

NORTHROP N-9M

Because the N-9Ms were seen as research tools, they were not given military serials. The all-yellow color scheme on the first machine (seen here) was replaced by medium blue undersurfaces and yellow uppersurfaces on the fourth aircraft, the N-9MB.

On the N-9MA those colors were repeated, but later reversed. The first aircraft crashed on May 19, 1943, but the N-9MB was restored and flown on November 11, 1994, almost 50 years after its first flight on January 26, 1945.

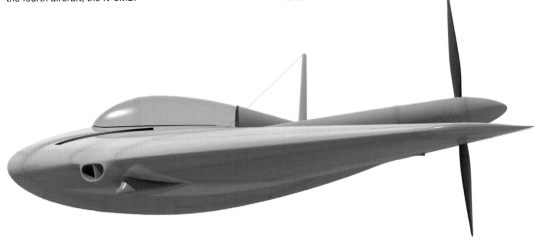

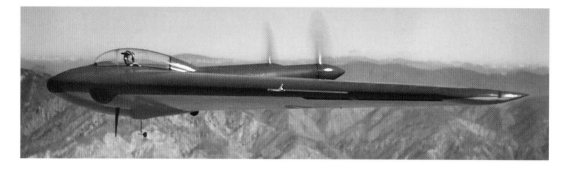

technical problems – mainly engine faults – causing early abandonment of 40 out of 44 flights. The final attempt, on May 19, 1943, for stability control flight, including stalls, ended in an elevon control reversal situation at a high AoA, with the cg situated towards the rear of the aircraft. The N-9M entered a nose-down spin over Rosamond Dry Lake and would not respond to the left anti-spin parachute (later found to be, in Jack Northrop's opinion "ineffective in size and improperly located"), which "streamered" in the airflow.

Although Constant jettisoned the canopy, set the propeller brakes and tried to bail out, it seems that the full-aft control column – a characteristic of flying wings in an uncommanded dive – pinned him into his seat and he was killed when the aircraft spun in. A hydraulic ram was subsequently installed to push the stick forward in such an emergency. Later tests showed that the effect of the rudders changed at high AoA above 34 degrees for the B-35 configuration. Directing the rudders into the spin, which normally enabled a recovery, worsened the situation at high AoA. Tests also showed that the aircraft could tumble "head over heels" if it entered a spin while pitching up and down beyond 34 degrees AoA. This was seen to be an unrecoverable situation.

However, tests also indicated that the N-9M had no inherently unacceptable control characteristics in normal flight, so N-9M-2 was duly flown on June 24, 1943. The brief flight was curtailed by a lost canopy. Engine problems continued, but some useful data was eventually recorded in September which showed that the XB-35's drag was likely to be around ten percent higher than expected, enabling Northrop to produce more accurate performance estimates.

Some control difficulties also persisted, partly because the N-9M was manually controlled. No hydraulic system was initially available, and the booster systems that were tested proved to be inadequate. It was found that control column forces were reversed, making the former produce pitch

The N-9M was provided with spring-loaded propeller locks so that a pilot would not be injured by a windmilling propeller if he had to bail out. The two-bladed propellers could be locked in the horizontal position to avoid damage to them in a wheels-up landing. The aircraft were painted in the company's distinctive yellow test scheme, although the N-9MA (seen here) was eventually given blue uppersurfaces in order to make it easier for observers (both on the ground and in the air) to see which way up it was flying if it looped or was rolled inverted. (Terry Panopalis collection)

The XB-35 mock-up, as seen on November 22, 1946, included the pilot's position, with its fairly basic flight instrumentation. The much more complex monitoring panels for the engines and systems were located in the flight engineer's part of the cabin. (Terry Panopalis collection)

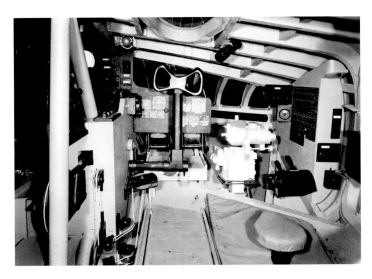

The co-pilot (his seat removed here in this mock-up) was positioned lower than the pilot (to his left). The bombing controls and sight are to his right in the bombardier's station. (Terry Panopalis collection)

The first XB-35, still unpainted, on April 30, 1946. Domed fairings represent the gun turret positions. Adjustable slots in the leading edge are open, as they would be to delay stalls at low speeds. Armed USAAF sentries have been posted to guard this valuable machine. (Terry Panopalis collection)

motions that were opposite to the norm as the aircraft neared a stall. Spin recovery was possible by ruddering into the spin. Northrop eventually installed a fully powered hydraulic system based on a series of small, sensitive valves, with artificial "feel" to even out the control forces and overcome this stick reversal.

The N-9M-2, which tested leading edge slats and "aero-boost" intakes in its leading edges, was slightly damaged in a belly landing in April 1944, although the N-9MA was available from April 20 to test control modifications that would appear in the XB-35. The pneumatic aero-boost involved air chambers and bellows to provide a gradual, automatic power boost for elevon operation as airspeed increased. It was rendered obsolete by the use of one of the earliest irreversible hydraulic controls with artificial pitch feel for the XB-35. Clamshell "rudders" were replaced by a split drag rudder built into the wing's outer trailing edge, and a pitch trimmer was also installed.

A fourth aircraft, the N-9MB, was built to replace the first N-9M, and it used 300hp Franklin XO-540-7 eight-cylinder engines in place of the unreliable Menascos of the first three examples. The aircraft also had an antenna mast behind the cockpit, fully powered hydraulic controls and slot doors in the wingtips. One benefit of the manually selected hydraulic boost was prevention of the conditions that had resulted in the death of Max Constant.

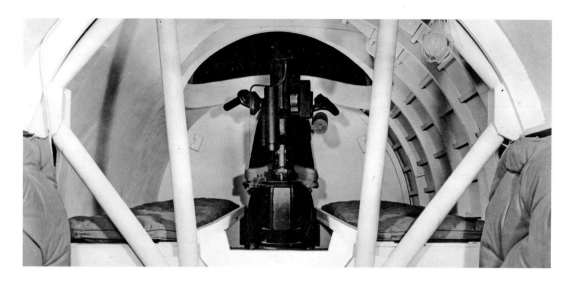

USAAF personnel test-flew the N-9MA in June and reported favorably on its handling characteristics as a prelude to a sustained 70-flight test series by AMC. When the program was complete the three N-9s were used to familiarize more than 20 USAAF pilots (including Capt Glen Edwards) with flying wing characteristics ahead of the B-35 order, and they also amassed further data for the bomber program. Development work on an autopilot, using a modified conventional unit for the flying wing, was also completed successfully with the N-9Ms. They were finally retired in mid-1947 and used for ground instruction at the Northrop Aeronautical Institute. The two-seat N-9MB was later restored in an eight-year project by volunteers, including many former Northrop employees, and flown by the Planes of Fame Museum at Chino, California.

The B-35 mock-up included the rear-upper gunner's position, accessed through part of the cabin that contained bunks for the long-range relief crew. A periscope gunsight was provided. (Terry Panopalis collection)

The first XB-35 on an early flight. Problems with the gearboxes, governors and propellers persisted during its test flights from July 3, 1946 to March 10, 1948. Gun turrets in the tail and wings were installed on the second aircraft, 42-38323. (Terry Panopalis collection)

LEFT
The XB-35's very unconventional structure is highlighted in this view of the asymmetric crew positions. The company's chief structural engineer, A. M. Schwartz, is standing on the pilot's seat. The canopy covering the cockpit offered no shelter from the desert sun, and test pilot Max Stanley described the cockpit as a "hothouse." (Terry Panopalis collection)

BIGGER BAT

Although lack of personnel and technical capacity had slowed the N-9 program, both Northrop and the USAAF were determined to pursue the B-35 project, described in Northrop publicity as its "monster new bat bomber". Northrop's original performance estimates included a range of up to 8,000 miles carrying 2,000lbs of bombs, rather than the USAAF's ambitious 10,000lbs load – the size of an atomic bomb at the time. He suggested an in-service date of 1944, only a year after the proposed introduction of the B-29 Superfortress, which would have a shorter range and inferior performance.

A mock-up of the thick center-section was built in Northrop's new Plant 3, and it contained an unusually spacious cabin with rest and sleeping areas containing six bunks for a long-range relief crew, a kitchen, and room for a tall man to stand. The crew included two pilots, a bombardier, a radio operator, a navigator, an engineer, and three gunners, whose remote sighting stations for the seven gun turrets would be in the tail-cone of production B-35s.

Northrop quickly began assembly of the first XB-35, pushing ahead in the hope of beating Consolidated's XB-36 for major contracts. Its massive 172ft wingspan included two hydraulic elevons (with electrical back-up) that were each 34.5ft long. The trailing edge area between each pair of gearbox nacelles acted as landing flaps. Using the trailing edge in this way inevitably reduced wing camber when the elevons were operated, slightly reducing lift and increasing take-off and landing speeds. Hydraulically-operated slots in the leading edges of the wingtips prevented wingtip stall at low speeds, but they were covered by shutters at higher speeds. They were operated by a three-position switch, giving manual or automatic control, and were normally open for landing and take-off or, at other times, automatically, depending on the wing's lift coefficient. Split rudder surfaces in the wingtips extended independently (operated by the pilot's rudder pedals) to act as "drag" rudders or together as airbrakes. Trim flaps at the wingtips helped to moderate the split flaps' tendency to pitch the aircraft downwards.

Four Pratt & Whitney R-4360 radial engines, also used in the Convair (formerly Consolidated) B-36, and promising an eventual power output of 4,000hp, were housed in the forward area of the wing, with complex cooling arrangements. Long shafts carried the drive to pairs of contra-rotating, four-bladed Hamilton Standard Super Hydromatic propellers via gearboxes built into housings on the trailing edge, which also provided some directional stability. A six-bladed propeller arrangement was ground-tested on one engine. Four main fuel tanks were connected by a common manifold. Each

auxiliary electrical power unit had its own 42-gallon fuel tank in the No. 5 bomb-bay, while the rest of the fuel for the R-4360s filled most of the outer wing space.

Defensive machine guns in shallow blister turrets above and below the wing and behind the pilot's canopy were operated by a gunner from a bubble-canopied position between the two central engine locations, and another four 0.50-cal weapons were to be fired remotely from an innovative, conical "stinger" turret in the tail. This consisted of two swiveling sections, and commanded a wide cone of fire without damaging the propellers. Gun turrets were fitted to the second XB-35 and the YB-35, while the first XB-35 had blisters in place of turrets.

Seated under a fixed bubble canopy, the pilot had good all-round vision except to the rear, and the co-pilot to his right looked forwards and downwards from the wing's leading edge. Both had control wheels and columns, but only the pilot had the visibility to land or take off. Airspeed dials, radio controls, and fuel quantity gauges were accessible from both positions. The flight engineer, navigator, radio operator, and bombardier occupied internal, windowless positions.

The bomber's heavy-duty electrically actuated tricycle undercarriage consisted of two twin-wheeled main units retracting forwards and a single, steerable nose-wheel that retracted to the left. Brakes were linked to the rudders – one of three "brake" switches had to be pressed and

The XB-35's massive, sideways-retracting nose landing gear echoed a similar unit in the Ho 229. The aircraft is seen here on August 4, 1947. (Terry Panopalis collection)

Northrop found a space to display the USAAF insignia and serial for the first XB-35, seen here en route to Muroc Army Air Field to begin flight tests on June 25, 1946 accompanied by a P-61 Black Widow. Max Stanley's view from the Plexiglas bubble canopy was good, but co-pilot Fred C. Brechter had more limited vision via the leading edge of the wing. Engineer Orva Douglas was kept busy deep inside the aircraft managing the fuel and Wasp Major engines. (Terry Panopalis collection)

The XB-35 had no automatic pilot as no suitable model was available, so it was hard to prevent slight instability in its directional axis if turbulence forced it off course – except by waiting for five or six lateral oscillations to correct themselves. On the first flight, landing gear retraction took almost a minute. (USAF)

held so that the rudder pedals would operate the brakes. Four throttles protruded from the cockpit roof, rather like the arrangement in some US Navy flying boats, and the engineer could control each powerplant individually.

Thirteen YB-35s were ordered in December 1942, followed in June 1943 by a contract for 200 production model B-35Bs to be manufactured by the Glenn L. Martin Company (which had already taken on much of the production engineering) in Baltimore, due to Northrop's limited production facilities. Martin was a somewhat negligent partner in the early stages of the deal, sub-contracting wing structure work to the Otis Elevator Company on the east coast and employing inadequate numbers of qualified staff on the project. Martin's management provided little support to its workforce, and time was wasted over duplication of effort and lack of communication between Hawthorne and the Martin plant.

NORTHROP XB-35 PROTOTYPE (continues overleaf)

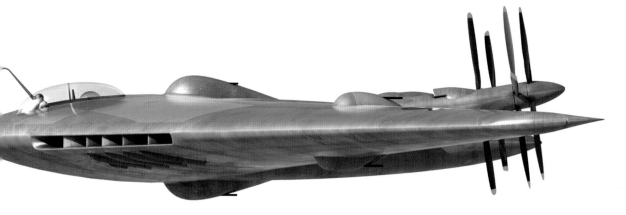

The prototype XB-35 took to the air for the first time on June 25, 1946 and made just 18 flights prior to returning to Hawthorne airfield and being placed in storage on October 7, 1948. It has the original double propeller arrangement, and the gun turret positions are faired over. Propeller spinners were fitted for most flights.

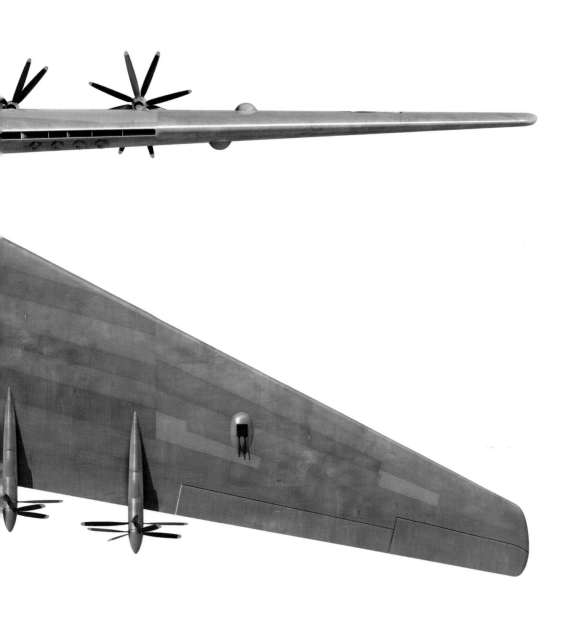

BAT BOMBER FLIES

Although Allied success in the war brought cancelation of the Martin contract on May 24, 1944, the project continued in prototype form; Northrop subsequently had to re-do much of Martin's abandoned engineering work. Pilot Max Stanley had signed on with Northrop on the understanding that he would not have to fly the XB-35, but Dr Sears asked him to do so and he soon developed a favorable impression of the huge aircraft.

The first example (42-13603) was ready to fly from Hawthorne's 5,000ft runway on a hot June 25, 1946 morning. Northrop employees had watched the largest land aircraft to have flown at that time being prepared for its first flight for almost a year, and many witnessed the take-off, despite a managerial edict that they should remain at work, as Jack Northrop himself did. As the plane accelerated, Max Stanley noticed a rabbit running ahead and outdistancing him, but the XB-35 eventually picked up speed and soared away towards Muroc to begin tests. Pilots soon got used to the rapid rate of climb, and the aircraft's pilot's manual advised, "Do not be alarmed at the nose-high attitude on take-off."

The XB-35 was already well behind schedule, and the cumulative delays over the summer probably cost the project valuable production time for the B-35s. Most of the problems concerned the engines, propeller governors, and gearboxes, including late delivery of these government-furnished equipment (GFE) items – an issue that was outside Northrop's control. Hamilton Standard had a huge workload of wartime contracts, limiting time for the complex new challenges of the XB-35's transmission and propellers. Jack Northrop noted that

The XB-35 at Hawthorne on April 30, 1946. Company employees had a chance to inspect the first XB-35 at the company's May 1946 Family's Day, when Jack Northrop spoke to the crowd. For nearly a year, they would have been aware of the aircraft parked on the pre-flight ramp at Hawthorne, as it awaited solutions to its propulsion problems. (Terry Panopalis collection)

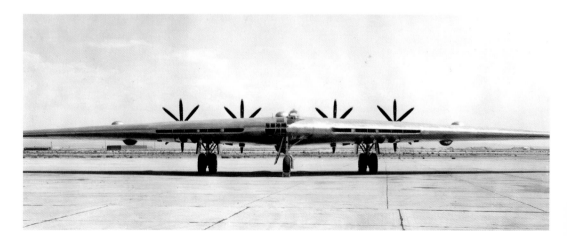

A rear view of the XB-35, with its original eight-bladed propeller system which provided a stabilizing effect that had to be reinstated in the jet-powered YB-49A with small vertical fins and strakes, much to Jack Northrop's disappointment. (Terry Panopalis collection)

LEFT
The XB-35, seen on October 13, 1947. For engine start-up, the engineer had to "inch each engine through two revolutions with the starter" and "engage and disengage the starter so that the engine is turned only a few degrees at a time." The APUs had to be started first, followed by a complex sequence involving control of turbo-boost, carburettors, intercooler temperature, gearbox temperature, cylinder head temperature, and throttles, as well as fuel management. Vibration in the engineer's instrument panel display area could make the dials hard to read accurately. (Terry Panopalis collection)

"six months, from August [1945] to March [1946], were spent in a vain attempt to eliminate these difficulties, plus those caused by a series of engine reduction gear failures. To date [May 1947] the XB-35 has not had sufficient time in the air to fully demonstrate its design performance guarantees."

It was particularly frustrating for him to see that repeated wind-tunnel tests confirmed the company's predictions on drag reduction, only for it to be unable to confirm them in flight and conduct the stability and maneuverability tests that should have been followed.

During the early tests at Muroc the team encountered vibrating drive shafts, overheating gearboxes, and propellers that would not feather correctly or maintain a constant speed. There were also frequent cases of oil leaks in the propeller governors, resulting in the aircraft often returning from test flights with one or more engines inoperative. It was small comfort to Northrop to know that the XB-36, which had first flown on August 8, 1946, was also experiencing serious engine overheating and propeller pitch problems, while its electric gun-turret system was proving to be so unreliable that it was eventually removed from the production B-36A.

It was also becoming clear that postwar budget constraints would not allow the purchase of two very costly new bombers, and reliability problems with the XB-35's propulsion systems gave Convair the advantage, because its technical maladies could be solved more quickly.

A USAAF AMC summary of the flight tests starkly revealed Northrop's difficulties, noting that on the second flight there was "erratic operation of the propeller governor No. 2," while governor No. 3 "hunted with a variation of about +/- 100 rpm." The pilot had difficulty in feathering the propellers during the third flight and the aircraft was then grounded because of propeller and gearbox difficulties. The No. 4 engine gearbox failed on the ninth flight, terminating it. Governor troubles and two propeller malfunctions recurred on flight No. 10. An emergency landing was made on the eleventh flight after partial failure of the No. 4 gearbox, and propeller vibration issues continued through 17 of its 18 total test flights up to March 10, 1948. Flight 12 was the only one to be declared "highly satisfactory."

YB-35 42-102366 in flight over the Mojave dry lakes. It first flew on May 12, 1948, and its last flight was only three months later. The original 1942 contract called for 13 YB-35s, but only one was completed. It carried the "buzz number" BG-366 under its left wing and had gun turrets installed. (Terry Panopalis collection)

After these disappointments Northrop suspended tests and demanded better government solutions to the power problems. Other equipment failures continued, including exhaust leaks and auxiliary power unit breakdowns, and the problems were carried over into the second aircraft (42-38323). This was flown for the first time, by Maj Bob Cardenas, on June 26, 1946, its first take-off being somewhat unexpected when a headwind gust lifted the aircraft off the runway early. The second aircraft made only eight flights in all, ending on September 11, 1946, by which point Northrop had removed the dual-rotating propeller system from both XB-35s, resorting to a single-rotation method with different gearboxes.

The first aircraft flight-tested this installation on February 12, 1948, a month after the second jet-powered YB-49 had flown. Single rotation only exacerbated the vibration problems, due to interference between the propellers, reducing performance and stability by disturbing the airflow over the rear of the wing. Speed reduction of about 30mph was common, as were vibration-induced cracks in the propeller housings and adjacent wing-ribs. Piston engines were nearing the end of their potential development in the constant search for more power, and the XB-35's R-4360s were very heavy on maintenance, with four dual magnetos, 56 spark plugs, and manually-adjusted valves for each engine. Despite all this, Northrop continued to advocate the B-35 as a faster, lighter, and more cost-effective alternative to the B-36, but six months of cumulative delays, caused mainly by engine problems, made that a fast-receding possibility.

The first XB-35 (42-13603) soaks up the sun at Muroc AAB. In tests it demonstrated a top speed of 346mph at 35,000ft – 8mph faster than the B-36A. It was re-designated as an ERB-35B in January 1949, reverting to the XB-35 title in June, but it was scrapped two months later. (Terry Panopalis collection)

JET SOLUTIONS

In other ways, the flying wing principle was constantly proven during the flight program, where N-9M test pilot Max Stanley demonstrated good stall recovery characteristics, excellent acceleration, and rate of climb impeded only by inconsistent engine power, which induced yawing. Jack Northrop admitted that no "violent maneuvers" were attempted during the tests, and he acknowledged that installing an autopilot would have had great advantages, but it was ruled out by the aircraft's side-slip characteristics. In any case, during 1944 Northrop, at the suggestion of the USAAF, had already begun to explore the use of jet engines to solve the propulsion difficulties.

In June 1945 the USAAF, anxious to save what seemed to be a failing project, modified its contract to allow the conversion of two YB-35s to use six or eight turbojets. This new version was initially designated YB-35B, preceding B-35B production versions, although there was some concern over the potential speed of a production jet-powered version, as the thick wing could cause excess drag and increased control problems at 500mph. Jet installation was to be a compromise that would allow little re-design of the airframe. The B-35 project really needed both jet engines and in-flight refueling, but the latter was only just becoming available in 1948 for B-50s, and never for the B-36, using the British system. Tanker squadrons were not established until 1949.

The first six YB-35s were to be completed with the single-rotation propeller system in an attempt to overcome the critical delays caused by ineffective GFE supplies. In December 1945 this decision was changed, allowing only the two jet-modified YB-35s (the second and third) to proceed, redesignated as YB-49s. The remaining airframes were to be held pending a decision on their future. Northrop had completed them on time, but the GFE engines, armament, auxiliary power units, and other crucial components were delayed, leaving a row of flying wing shells at Hawthorne.

XB-35 Technical Specifications

Wingspan – 172ft
Leading edge sweep – 27 degrees
Wing area – 4,000sq ft
Wing loading – 45lb/ft^2
Height – 30ft 3in.
Length – 53ft 1in.
Powerplants – four Pratt & Whitney R-4360-17 or -21 Wasp major supercharged 28-cylinder, four-row, air-cooled radial engines (two of each variant, which were the same, apart from drive shafts of different lengths) developing 3,000hp each. Each engine had two contra-rotating, four-bladed propellers. A three-bladed pair was also tested. Air-cooling came from slots in the wings' leading edges. Fuel capacity was 8,000 gallons.
Operational altitude – 40,000ft
Maximum speed – 391mph
Cruising speed – 240mph
Range – 7,500 miles
Empty weight (with gun turrets) – 91,000lbs
Gross weight – 154,000lbs
Maximum take-off weight – 209,000lbs
Proposed bomb-load (typical for operational version) – 16,000lbs in eight bomb-bays, rather than six bays in the XB-35. The largest of the bays were 12ft 4in. long, 4ft 4in. wide, and 6ft 6in. deep, but they could not accommodate the large 12,000lb conventional bombs or nuclear weapons that the USAAF wanted to carry.
Proposed defensive armament – six remote turrets with 0.50-cal M2 machine guns located above and below the tail section and above and below the outer wings, operated by gunners from four transparent observation domes. Up to 20 guns were to be carried in all, each with 1,000 rounds.
Notes – The XB-35 structure was advanced in choice of materials as well as aerodynamics, using innovative, stronger 75ST type aluminum and Roebling-made Alclad control cables. Its 3,000hp engines, transmission, and Hamilton Standard propellers used drive shafts that were almost 30ft long, coupled to complex gearboxes. The 62 engine and fuel gauge instruments were monitored by the engineer in a rear-facing compartment 10ft behind the pilot with no external view. The navigator was situated beside him and the co-pilot's seat gave a forward view from the wing's leading edge. Later USAF evaluation of the YB-49 version questioned the usefulness of the co-pilot, due to his restricted view and access to the cockpit instruments, recommending that he should be re-located in a Boeing B-47-type tandem cockpit behind the pilot beneath a jettisonable Plexiglas canopy with a conventional windshield.

The end of World War II inevitably brought a rapid decline in aircraft orders, slow supply of components, and many cancelations. Although new technologies would provide future opportunities, employment prospects in the industry were fewer in 1946. For Northrop, this meant the loss of influential senior figures to other companies, including La Motte T. Cohu, who initially went to TWA and then became President of Consolidated Vultee, where he attracted many Northrop managers to work with him. Moye Stephens, Dr William Sears, and sales vice-president Ted Coleman also departed.

Northrop's B-35 contract included a YB-35 (42-102366) that would have been the definitive pre-production item. Featuring the single-rotation propeller system and some of the defensive armament, its first flight was performed on May 15, 1948, but no other test flights were recorded for it.

A second YB-35A was redesignated ERB-35B (later, EB-35B), and work began to equip it with Northrop Turbodyne XT-37 turboprops. These were initially developed in partnership with the California-based Joshua-Hendy Company as another attempt to remedy the propulsion faults. Northrop had rejected a similar offer from General Electric, but disappointment with Joshua-Hendy led him to cancel the arrangement and set up the Northrop-owned Turbodyne Corporation in 1949. In January 1949 it was intended to fit a single XT-37 alongside six J35-A-19 turbojets, adding a second XT-37 later. Designed by Vladimir

Pavlecka with Jack Northrop, the XT-37 originated as a jet engine in the 1930s and was developed after the former had joined Northrop in 1939. Development was taken over by Art Phelan, initially for a US Navy contract, and he converted the axial-flow jet into a turbo-prop, developing 5,150hp in 1947, as the first working US turboprop.

As a pusher unit the turboprop jet exhaust would have vented through the propeller blades. In the EB-35B, converted from the first XB-35 (rather than from a YB-35A, which was re-assigned as the YRB-49A prototype), two XT-37s would have driven double propellers similar to those in the XB-35, and additional power would have come from four J35A-19 turbojets. For long-distance cruise flight, it was calculated that the aircraft could extend its range considerably by relying on the turboprop and throttling back the turbojets. The jets would then be powered up for take-off or high-speed dash, giving the EB-35 performance that included a range of up to 12,000 miles – real competition for the B-36.

Northrop's belief in the power and fuel economy of the Turbodyne continued throughout the years in which he promoted his large flying wing designs. It was listed as a possible alternative to jet power in the Boeing B-52, and suggested as the powerplant for the B-36, rather than its Pratt & Whitney R-4360 piston engines.

After only 27 flights totaling 36 hours and 19 minutes of flying time, both XB-35s were placed in storage at Hawthorne in January 1949. By the end of August, they and two YB-35s (42-102366 and 42-102369) had been scrapped, including the only one to have flown. It was hoped that the other YB-35s could be converted to jet power after flight tests by YB-49s, and that finance would also be available to proceed with the EB-35B and the YRB-49A reconnaissance version.

The distance between the XB-35's engine locations and its propeller system, driven by long shafts, is indicated by the exhaust and oil stains on its multi-metallic exterior. (USAF)

CHAPTER FOUR

JET WINGS

Conversion of the XB-35 to jet-powered YB-49 configuration was relatively straightforward, requiring only new engine mountings, air intakes, fuel lines, and engine monitoring instruments. Four small fins were also added above and below the trailing edge to restore the stability previously imparted by the propellers and gearbox covers. Wing fences extended those fins forward to prevent span-wise flow of boundary layer air, but the XB-35 control system remained substantially unchanged. Jet power almost eliminated the vibration experienced in the XB-35, although the ventral fins were subjected to some turbulence when the landing gear was lowered.

No fewer than eight J35-A-5 engines were needed because of their relatively low thrust, and like other GFE for the project, they and their new constant-speed drives were delayed. Fuel storage for the thirsty turbojets – the most powerful available at the time – was also increased. Five high-pressure hydraulic systems were used, four of them classified as Power Boost systems, to operate the various flying controls. Two more were required for the landing gear, brakes, and other functions. Pilots' escape hatches were provided above their positions and in the floor behind them. Other crew members could leave through a floor hatch in the crew nacelle, although exit through the open bomb-bay was recommended as the best way of clearing the aircraft.

Significant reductions in drag helped to increase the cruising speed to 365mph, and added 100mph to the maximum speed, but at a 50 percent cost in range, due to the increased fuel consumption. Removing the wing-mounted gun turrets reduced the crew to seven, and a further USAF review deleted the four-gun tail turret as well.

The YB-49 cruises over the Mojave Desert, where most of its flight testing took place. The pilot of the aircraft had only two throttle levers, each of which controlled four engines (the left or right bank of four). Control of individual engines could only be done by the flight engineer. Typically, the outboard split trim flaps, doubling as rudders and airbrakes, are slightly open for stability. (Terry Panopalis collection)

This November 22, 1946 view of a section of wing structure, common to both the XB-35 and the YB-49, shows the depth of the interior space even in the outer wing area. The circular aperture is a gun turret location. (Terry Panopalis collection)

It seemed to Northrop that the XB-35 had been a design just waiting for jet power to be available, and it transformed what Sir Frederick Handley Page called Northrop's "great thought" into the flying wing that Jack had always envisaged. However, the performance improvements brought the consequent possibilities of over-stressing the airframe, and no structural changes were funded to allow for this. There was also concern over the thickness of the wing, which, at higher speeds, would cause the airflow to separate from the surface too early, making the control surfaces less effective.

After delays in delivery of the engines, constant speed drives, and other GFE items, Max Stanley, with co-pilot Fred C. Bretcher and engineer Orva Douglas, who also crewed the maiden XB-35 flight, took the YB-49 (42-102367) aloft for the first time on October 21, 1947 when they flew the bomber from Hawthorne to Muroc Air Force Base (AFB). Stanley noticed the lack of vibration compared with the XB-35, and that the new aircraft's increased acceleration after take-off required the slow-operating landing gear units to be retracted promptly to avoid damage to their unmodified doors.

There were also frequent failures in the Franklin 37.5KVa auxiliary power units (APU) located in bomb-bays Nos. 3 and 6 (a common problem with the XB-35 and other experimental aircraft at that time) and a shortage of the units. It was also reported that reliance on APUs for all of the aircraft's alternating current electric power limited its altitude to 40,000ft, with consequent range reduction. If cabin pressure

The first YB-49 (42-102367) nears completion. The vertical fins and their continuation fences border the neat installation of eight J35 engines. In the bewildering sequence of changing designations that affected the series, this aircraft was originally a YB-35, but was re-designated as an XB-35 on November 18, 1944, finally becoming a YB-49 on June 12, 1945 after conversion. Accepted by the USAF on May 25, 1949, it was lost in a high-speed taxiing accident on March 15, 1950. (Terry Panopalis collection)

failed above 20,000ft, caused in two cases by the loss of a bubble canopy, the cabin air that helped to power the APUs was lost and they cut out. The vulnerability of the canopies under pressure became another reason for the 40,000ft ceiling, although the aircraft could have gone higher. Overall though, Stanley rated the XB-49 as "an absolute joy to fly," and asserted that there was "no comparison" with the propeller-driven XB-35.

Some of Stanley's flights out over the Pacific revealed one of the aircraft's unsuspected and (at the time) undervalued properties. As he approached the coast near San Francisco, it became apparent that the early warning radar station at Half Moon Bay was unable to detect him. The slender flying wing cross-section was invisible until the aircraft was almost overhead. Thirty years later, a fuller understanding of what came to be known as stealth, combined with Northrop's flying wing experience, would give the company the lead in designing the B-2 Spirit bomber.

On January 13, 1948 Stanley gave Jack Northrop his first trip in the new aircraft, which was the largest and most powerful jet bomber in the world at the time. That same day the second YB-49 (42-102368) also made its maiden flight, although en route to Muroc it suffered an APU fault, causing undercarriage extension problems. An intensive program totaling 330 flight hours followed, revealing that the higher fuel consumption reduced range considerably, allowing less than 4,000 miles with a 10,000lb bomb-load – far short of the USAF requirement. Although in-flight refueling was used by some B-29 and B-50 bombers in 1948, and the USAF considered it an urgent priority, it was not available operationally until late 1949, and never for the YB-49.

The first YB-49 takes off at the start of its maiden flight on October 21, 1947, with Max Stanley, Fred C. Bretcher, and Orva Douglas as the crew. Its slow gear retraction (averaging around 90 seconds) and rapid acceleration on take-off required a steep AoA to avoid exceeding the speed limitations for an extended undercarriage. The engines left long black smoke-trails as they developed full power, which only reduced when the pilot throttled back. One of the aircraft's advertised advantages was its minimal hangar requirement, as it could be placed on dollies and towed sideways into a long, thin hangar building. Its closeness to the ground also made for easier maintenance, as most of it could be reached from low platforms and ladders. It was the exact opposite in this respect to SAC's later bomber project, the XB-70 Valkyrie. (Terry Panopalis collection)

Jack Northrop's idea of a clean airframe was better realized in the YB-49 (the first example is seen here), without the piston engines, gun turrets, and other projections of the XB-35. With the approval of AMC, Northrop chose to avoid the XB-49 label for the new aircraft on the supposition that the basic concept had been proven by the XB-35 and the aircraft could go straight to the pre-production, service test stage with a "YB" prefix. It also reflected the company's urgent need of a production contract. (Terry Panopalis collection)

PHASE TWO

Maj Robert Cardenas, the officer in charge of Flight Test Division projects at Muroc and the USAF's assigned test pilot for the YB-49, checked out in the first prototype on December 2, 1947 after diverting to head the Bell X-1 project while it made its successful attempt to break the "sound barrier." Cardenas had been critical of the aerodynamics of the XB-35, with its trailing-edge propellers suffering from flutter as they coped with air masses coming over and under the wing at different velocities and temperatures. In the YB-49 he noticed that after a maneuver the nose tended to make small Dutch roll movements. Following several trouble-free flights, Cardenas made a series of low-speed stall tests and recorded the experience in a report for the USAF. His main recommendation was that the YB-49 should provide stall warning, since he had completely and unexpectedly lost control. There were none of the usual aerodynamic "nibbles" experienced in other aircraft to indicate an imminent stall.

Max Stanley had begun to perform stall tests, but exploration of the more severe conditions (that were unlikely to be encountered in operational use) were curtailed, partly because he realized that there was no way to escape from the prototype aircraft in a steep stall/spin state. However, the USAF still wanted a large jet bomber to test the possibilities of the concept, and in 1947 the YB-49 was the only option.

Cardenas described the subsequent YB-49 stall test with Maj Danny Forbes Jr as "the ride of my life." Throttling back to idle at 20,000ft, he slowed to around 80kts until the nose suddenly dipped into a negative-G tumble, with no means of stopping it with the normal flying controls. With difficulty, he reached above him for the throttle handle for the four left engines, pushing them to full power. The bomber cart-wheeled and entered an inverted spin, from which Cardenas was finally able to recover at an altitude of only 800ft. It was calculated that the YB-49 lost 1,800ft for every turn in a spin. In his report, recommending that no further stall testing was necessary, Cardenas stated that, "This aircraft is never to be intentionally stalled," adding that there was usually no need to do so anyway. He praised many of its characteristics, describing it in later interviews as "a pleasurable airplane to fly." Cardenas also commented on its ease of landing. However, after his alarming stall experience, he did drive to Pancho Barnes' legendary "Fly Inn" bar, a retreat for most Muroc test pilots, that evening for a drink or two.

The second YB-49 was passed to the USAF on May 28, 1948 for familiarization flights by USAF personnel as concerns mounted about its future. It had already made 20 flights with company test pilots. There were undercarriage problems on several occasions, and on flight No. 11 the aft bubble canopy came off at 35,000ft, depressurizing the cabin area. Seven satisfactory bomb-drop runs were made during four flights in March, one of which was declared "highly successful." There were some encouraging demonstrations of the YB-49's speed and range capabilities too. On April 26 it flew a 3,007-mile test circuit lasting nine and a half hours with a 6,000lb dummy bomb-load at an average speed of 330mph – a record for a jet aircraft.

Despite several impressive endurance flights, six of them above 40,000ft, AMC was losing faith in the YB-49 as a combat aircraft, partly because its inherent instability was still apparent. There was no auto-stabilization system available to dampen it out and no suitable government-supplied autopilot to cope with the aircraft's unique aerodynamics, although there was an obvious need for one. The second aircraft did have a test version fitted.

FLYING WING DOWN

On May 19, 1948 Capt Glen W. Edwards went to Muroc to run USAF stability checks on the YB-49 and Phase II (service) tests on the XB-35. His master's degree in stability and control was essential for the tests, as test pilot Maj Danny Forbes had not completed the USAF Flight Test Division's stability and control course. Maj Cardenas (rather than a Northrop test pilot) had checked out Capt Edwards, a good friend and his Operations Officer in the USAF's Bomber Test Branch, on the YB-49 on May 20–21. It was an unusually difficult task because the seating arrangements placed the pilot and co-pilot at different levels. Both had flown the N-9M.

As an expert on the subject, Capt Edwards noted that "stability is poor all round," but in Ted Coleman's view these criticisms were not discussed with Max Stanley or other company pilots, and no advice was sought from Northrop. Maj Cardenas strongly denied this assertion, stating that he personally had spent weekends with Max Stanley discussing the XB-49, and this was supported by Edwards' diary entries.

Edwards visited Hawthorne on May 26 to inspect the YRB-49A mock-up, returning to Muroc the next day to make two more

YB-49 test flights. He later noted that the aircraft became "quite uncontrollable at times" when he allowed it to enter a stall. Edwards realized that take-offs and coordinated turns required "a few hours' practice." A flying wing's steep take-off AoA and rapid nose-down acceleration compared with "normal" aircraft also required some pilot familiarization. Cardenas then left the program to get married and begin his two years of studies at the University of Southern California. He had to leave Edwards in charge of the program, although the latter had only three hours flying time on the YB-49 and the USAF had not requested a check flight for him from Max Stanley, who made the final company flight of the YB-49 program on May 27.

The following day Forbes and Edwards flew the second YB-49 for more than seven hours, testing airspeed, side-slips, and dives at 470mph (Mach 0.60). Edwards flew another four hours of stability tests on June 3, including further stall tests. Col Albert Boyd, head of flight testing at Wright Field, also flew the aircraft on this date and was apparently unimpressed. Like Glen Edwards, he thought it was a "passable airplane in ideal conditions." Edwards, who had spent many hours at the controls of other jet bombers, such as the Convair XB-46, noted that he did not like the YB-49 cockpit arrangement at all when he first inspected the plane.

Although no detailed flight plan was provided for flight No. 25 on June 5, 1948, it was apparently intended as an extra three-hour sortie to examine longitudinal stability at high AoA with two extra observers from Wright Field aboard. The second YB-49's rate of climb to its 40,000ft APU-limited service ceiling for speed tests at various power settings was probably to be checked. Forbes said in conversation the previous day that he intended to perform low-powered stall tests at 15,000ft, increasing the power gradually over a series of stalls. Power and fuel consumption tests with various engine combinations were then scheduled. The crew were pilot Maj Danny Forbes, Capt Glen Edwards as co-pilot and Lt Edward Swindell as flight engineer. Two highly-qualified civilian flight engineers on USAF contracts, Clare C. Leser and Charles LaFountain, were also aboard.

NORTHROP YB-49 PROTOTYPE (continues overleaf)

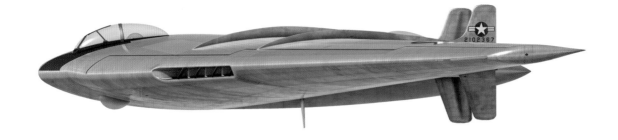

The first example of the YB-49, with its eight J35-A-15 engines and small but necessary vertical fins as the only impediment to Jack Northrop's ideal flying wing format. This aircraft conducted a full, successful program of 144 flights for Northrop and USAF tests between October 21, 1947 and March 15, 1950, when it was destroyed during a high-speed taxi trial. The XB-47, which first flew two months after the YB-49, was 80mph faster, although the Flying Wing's typical unrefueled range with a 10,000lb weapon load was 1,350 miles longer.

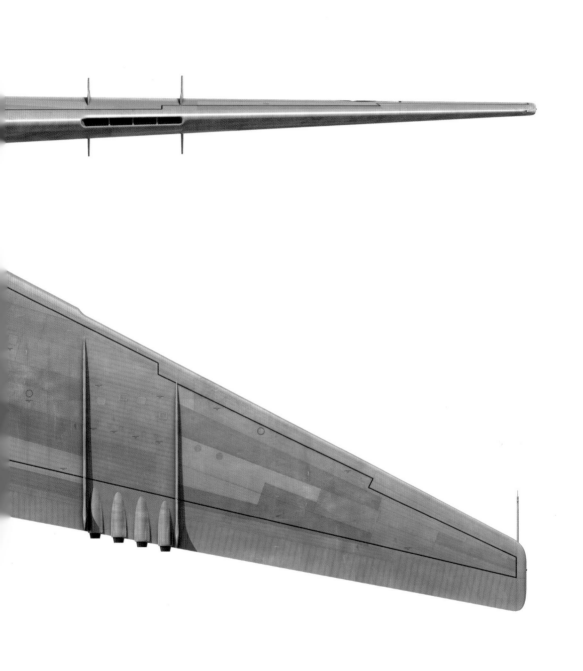

YB-49 42-102368 headed out from Muroc AFB at 0655 hrs on June 5, but apparently it did not reach the maximum altitude, and so the crew probably began stall tests. After about an hour with Maj Forbes at the controls it crashed 12 miles northwest of Muroc, hitting the ground flat and inverted and exploding in a fireball, with a 500ft smoke column from 9,000 gallons of remaining fuel. Flames destroyed most of the wreckage. There were no survivors. The crew had possibly perished under negative g-forces of up to -15 as the broken airframe tumbled down. The lack of ejection seats would have made escape in those conditions virtually impossible in any case.

Although no chase aircraft was available for the flight (it was a Saturday), eye-witnesses had seen the aircraft tumbling laterally, and one, Maj Russ E. Schleeh, saw what appeared to be a large piece of metal falling after the main airframe. Subsequent investigation indicated that the engines had been idling at the time of impact, and that both outer wings had bent upwards and broken off together, landing three miles from the main body. Some of the lightly-constructed control surfaces, including one rudder, had also separated and appeared to have been torn off while the aircraft was slipping backwards in a tumbling motion. All the fins had come off.

Various theories were advanced to explain the accident, but it was attributed to unexplained structural failure, possibly because the wing was over-stressed in an attempt to recover from a dive or spin that

The YB-49's nose-gear door was blown off as the aircraft climbed away from take-off at 280 knots on its second flight, disturbing the Delco electrical retraction system. Max Stanley resorted to the gravity-operated emergency gear extension system after an hour attempting to get the nose-wheel down. It forced the hefty nose-gear through its other closed doors and a safe landing was made. The usual advice from the flight engineer/electrician was lacking on this occasion as he had been injured while bailing out of a "chase" P-61. (Terry Panopalis collection)

The first YB-49 (42-102367) takes on a load of JP-1 fuel for its four main tanks (each one supplying two engines) and ten auxiliary or bomb-bay feeder tanks, all of which had a combined total capacity of 14,542 gallons. Seated behind the pilots, the flight engineer had the very complex task of managing all the engines and the fuel flow, ensuring that the tanks' contents were balanced to avoid cg problems. (Terry Panapolis collection)

LEFT
The first YB-49 at Muroc being prepared for another test flight, with the Douglas XB-43 in the background (left). USAF analysis also drew attention to the XB-49's uncomfortable crew seats, ineffective cabin heating on long flights, the co-pilot's limited view (a small area ahead and downwards) and the pilot's restricted view of the instrument panel, as the right side was only completely visible to the co-pilot. It recommended tandem seating like the B-47 Stratojet's. Control forces for the elevons were considered too light and the lack of full investigation of stall characteristics was criticized. No doubt these prototype problems, including modification of the bomb-bay doors, could have been corrected in a production model, but the USAF lacked the extra funding. (USAF)

started with insufficient altitude for safe recovery. In Jack Northrop's opinion, the stall tests left them only 7,500ft of clearance and less than two minutes in which to recover from a dive. He thought Forbes must have reacted to the aircraft's rapid downward acceleration by pulling out too suddenly and breaking off the outer wing panels. Other pilots had remarked on the light stick forces needed to control the YB-49, and the ease with which it could be over-stressed by its powerful hydraulics. They also noticed that, unlike most other aircraft, it gave no warning of an impending stall, and there was no AoA gauge to back up their calculated guesses at how steeply the aircraft was angled.

Wind-tunnel tests had shown that use of the rudders to curtail a spin actually made it worse, although correct use of the elevons could work. This information may not have been assimilated by the USAF crews at the time; its worth was demonstrated by Northrop pilot Chuck Tucker later that year when he recovered from a full stall using elevons only. He also had the landing gear lowered to help with speed reduction, as well as 30 percent aft cg achieved by shifting fuel around the tank system. Tucker ridiculed the accusations that the aircraft was uncontrollable, and found great difficulty in inducing a stall at 30,000ft, but when it happened at around 140mph it was sudden. The nose would rise, even with full aft elevon control, and the aircraft fell away to the right. Applying right rudder, rather than leaving the rudders alone, converted a stall to a near-vertical spin, from which he recovered after two turns, pulling out at 2.5g and 8,000ft without damage.

Forbes had apparently pulled up at more than 4g. Later tests showed that the airframe would break up at under 4.8g, and it was possible to pull 5g at quite low speeds. The definitive YB-49 pilot's handbook stated bluntly that, based on wind-tunnel data, "Intentional spins are prohibited in this airplane. There is no tendency for the aircraft to spin inadvertently in either the cruising or landing attitude. A roll from a stall may develop into a spin particularly with a rearward cg. An

airspeed of at least 20mph above the stall speed should be maintained at all times." It added that "abrupt pull-outs at high speeds should be avoided."

AMC also had reservations about the flying wing's cockpit canopy, with its internal plate glass windscreen and the poor access to emergency exits. Cardenas reported that "There were two aircraft, one instrumented for performance, the other for stability and control. Danny Forbes flew left seat on some performance flights (every third flight). We didn't wear parachutes because the canopy could not be jettisoned and there was no seat ejection. To bail out, you had to rotate the seat, jack it down four feet, walk back to the hatch, put on the parachute there and drop out."

Contractor (Interim Phase 1) tests recommenced on July 21, 1948 after the remaining YB-49 was grounded following the June 5 crash because, as Jack Northrop stated, the USAF insisted on the aircraft repeating all of its pre-crash acceptance tests. The memory of the lost crew was honoured with the re-naming of bases in the pilots' home states. Topeka AFB, Kansas, became Forbes AFB in June 1949, and Muroc AFB, California, was re-named Edwards AFB in January 1950.

Although the glazed nose of the XB-35 and YB-49 offered an unusual downward and forward view, the bombsight and instrument panels in front of the co-pilot and bombardier tended to limit their vision. This photograph of the YB-49's crew area was taken in May 1948 at Muroc. (Terry Panopalis collection)

The YB-49, in this case seemingly pursued by its nemesis, a Carswell AFB-based B-36A-5-CF (44-92010), at Andrews AFB in February 1949 for Congressional inspection. The B-36's gigantic dimensions gave rise to many stories, including one from a groundcrewman who asked to be driven out to a B-36 so that he could deal with an engine problem. His driver then asked him which part of the aircraft he would like to be driven to. (USAF)

BOMBING WING

In March 1948 the second YB-49 was fitted with bomb racks for conventional ordnance. Pinpoint accuracy was obviously not required for nuclear delivery, which was the main point of purchasing a new long-range bomber, although the YB-49 could not carry contemporary nuclear weapons. Seven satisfactory bomb-drop runs were made during four flights that month, one of which was declared "highly successful," but others were interrupted by bad weather or bomb-bay door problems.

The USAF's bombing tests resumed in October 1948, and they directly compared the Northrop bomber with a B-29 as manually-operated bombers without autopilots, although an advanced autopilot for fast jet bombers was being developed and the simple autopilot used in the N-9M had been quite effective in controlling yaw. The only available YB-49 autopilot was lost in the crash of 42-102368 prior to the aircraft having tested its performance when loaded with weaponry.

The first YB-49 achieved half the B-29's accuracy with M38 100lb practice bombs and M64 500lb inert ordnance and took up to four minutes for the pilot to stabilize on the bomb run, correcting the aircraft's slight tendency to yaw, compared with 45 seconds for the Boeing bomber. Partly, this was because the USAF fitted the standard Norden bombsight, a complex device originating in 1928 that required an extremely stable aircraft as its platform, for the trials. The B-29 used a Norden, so the same sight had to be installed in the YB-49, even though it was far from ideal.

Maj Cardenas, pilot for the bombing trials, reported that the YB-49 displayed marginal stability about all three axes and phugoid oscillations (slow and fairly gentle Dutch rolls) in turns or when climbing and diving. He was at pains to point out that he never described the aircraft as "unstable," but "marginally stable, yawing a degree or two to each side," adding that Northrop had "a beautiful concept that was 20 years ahead of its time." In his view it was not an operational weapons system, but a design waiting for technology to catch up with it and provide the computers, auto-stabilization, and cockpit escape systems that it required. AMC's analysis seriously overstated the situation in Cardenas' opinion, describing the YB-49 in a summary report as "extremely unstable and very difficult to fly on a bombing mission" and "unsuitable for either bomber or reconnaissance work." Cardenas saw this as a gross exaggeration of his comments.

In later bombing tests in June 1949 the YB-49 was briefly linked to a yaw-damping Minneapolis Honeywell E-7 "Little Herbert" autopilot that apparently improved accuracy and, in Max Stanley's opinion, "essentially corrected the problem." According to AMC, bomb release and accuracy were still erratic, and the proposed K-1 optical and radar bombsite, that would have been a better match than the Norden, was never fitted. Test pilot Maj Schleeh reported that bombs fell into airflow that was apparently disturbed by turbulence in the bomb-bay, but he felt that this could have been cured, given time and money. Clearly the USAF, which had already ordered its first batch of B-47 Stratojets, was reluctant to provide more of either.

The YB-49's bomb-carrying capacity, without a cavernous bomb-bay like the B-36's, was also considered inadequate for contemporary "special" weapons. Northrop arranged eight weapons bays inboard of the XB-35's engines, but none could accommodate the 10,300lb Mk 3 "Fat Man" nuclear weapons used over Nagasaki, Japan. Two bays were deleted to accommodate extra fuel tanks when jet power was adopted, reducing the bomb load below the B-29's. In the original USAAF specification Northrop had understood that the biggest bomb to be carried would weigh only 4,000lbs. However, the first H-bombs for B-36s weighed 43,000lbs and were 30ft long. Also, the unusual thin metal "roll top" bomb doors that were wound on and off a drum, rather than extending below the aircraft in the usual way, were fragile when used in the faster YB-49 and sometimes refused to open during the bombing trials.

To cope with larger bombs, Northrop proposed that production B-49s could be modified to be nuclear-capable. He outlined external carriage for two large weapons, including T-14 22,000lb "bunker busters," but conceded severe performance penalties from weight and drag. The smaller 10,800lb Mk 4 atomic bomb (128in. long and 60in. in diameter) would have fitted into the bay of a B-35 or B-49, but only with complex structural alterations. These factors, and the aircraft's reduced range, brought reclassification as a medium bomber, ruling out competition with the B-36. Its more serious long-term competitor, the jet-powered B-47, was also considered a medium bomber, although it could carry larger "special" weapons and was 100mph faster.

Two bombers with quite different design philosophies. The B-47 Stratojet (right) replaced the B-49 in the USAF's medium bomber category due mainly to its speed and atomic weapons capability. It was so streamlined that landing required a 16ft parachute, deployed on approach to slow the aircraft, and a 32ft braking parachute for use after touch-down. Early versions could out-climb a MiG-15, but the fighter-type tandem cockpit meant that pilots could not monitor each other's actions. The B-47 brought radical innovations to bomber design, including its bicycle undercarriage, necessitated by the lack of storage space for the landing gear in the high-mounted wings. This arrangement required take-off and landing at a fixed, no flare attitude, and the risk of "porpoise" landings if one landing gear touched down before the other. Many accidents were attributed to its challenging flight characteristics, particularly on landing. Although the B-47's performance was significantly better than its predecessors, the aircraft's relatively low-powered J47 engines – like most early turbojets – suffered from poor fuel economy. This left the B-47 dependent on recently-introduced in-flight refueling. (Terry Panopalis collection)

YB-49 Technical Specifications

Wingspan – 172ft
Wing area – 4,000ft²
Length – 53ft 08in.
Height – 14.98ft
Elevon span – 34.5ft each
Powerplant – eight General Electric-designed Allison YJ35-A-15 (six J35-A-19 in YRB-49A) turbojets developing 3,750lbs thrust each
Weight – (empty) 80,122lbs, (loaded) 205,000lbs, (gross) 213,938lbs

Maximum speed – 428mph
Cruising speed – 365mph
Service ceiling – 42,000ft
Range – 2,828 miles with 10,000lbs of bombs
Defensive armament – 4 x 0.50-cal M2 machine guns in a remote-controlled "stinger" tail turret (deleted from YB-49 and YRB-49A design in January 1947)

The wing area of the B-35 and B-49, at 4,500ft², was 500ft² larger than that of the B-52 and Avro Vulcan, and swept back at 26.5 degrees. However, a 1955-era B-52D's maximum take-off weight was more than twice that of the YB-49's 213,500lbs, and its eight J57 engines developed 97,000lbs of combined thrust, compared with the 30,000lbs of the Flying Wing's eight J35s. (Terry Panopalis)

Only one officer from the USAF's senior General Staff, Eighth Air Force commander Gen Roger Ramey, flew in the YB-49 – he declared it a "fine ship with a real future." He was supported by Gen "Hap" Arnold and Strategic Air Command's (SAC) first commander, Gen George Kenney. For many of their colleagues, including the highly influential SAC chief from 1948, Gen Curtis LeMay, who, unlike Gen Kenney, doubted the whole flying wing idea and was convinced that it could not carry atomic bombs, that "real future" was decidedly insecure. The immediate problems, however, still lay with GFE items, particularly the engines and APUs.

It seemed to Northrop that the USAF was looking for excuses to undermine the project, although it was recognized that the YB-49 was still a test aircraft and far from reaching operational configuration. However, the erroneous but widely circulated conclusion that the aircraft was "unstable" was the most damaging element in the USAF's final judgement that, although the YB-49's problems might be solved in due course, it had already been overtaken by the faster B-47 Stratojet and its planned successor, the B-52 Stratofortress.

As a final decision on its fate neared, YB-49 42-102367 performed a limited public tour by order of Gen Ben Funk, deputy chief of the Aircraft Procurement Division at AMC Headquarters, including a January 1949 airshow at Andrews Field, Maryland, where it appeared alongside the XB-47. It made that leg of the trip at an impressive 511mph average speed, despite severe weather en route, although the XB-47 covered the same section of the route averaging 607mph. At Andrews, President Harry S. Truman inspected the

INSIDE THE NORTHROP YRB-49

A cutaway view from the left side of YRB-49

1. Camera control panel
2. Pilot's station
3. Radar navigator's station
4. Co-pilot's station
5. Flight engineer's station
6. Engine and fuel controls
7. Turret well (unused)
8. Portable oxygen cylinders
9. Center crew nacelle
10. Aft crew nacelle
11. Provision for mounting A-14 film magazine and amplifier
12. Stabilized vertical camera station
13. Trimetragon camera station
14. Storage racks
15. AN/APQ-24 radome fairing
16. Multiple camera station (aft)
17. Equipment stowage
18. 18in. split vertical camera station (alternative)
19. Central escape hatch
20. Multiple camera station (vertical)
21. Entrance ladder (stowed)
22. Photo-flash bomb-bay
23. Jugs for hot beverages (not visible here)
24. Radio operating station
25. Battery (in nosewheel well)
26. Nose landing gear doors bungee air bottles
27. Emergency brake air bottle
28. Photo navigator's station (on right side of cabin)
29. Type B-2 viewfinder
30. Forward oblique camera station

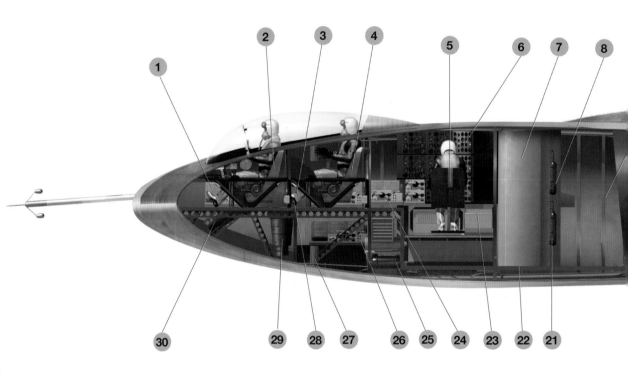

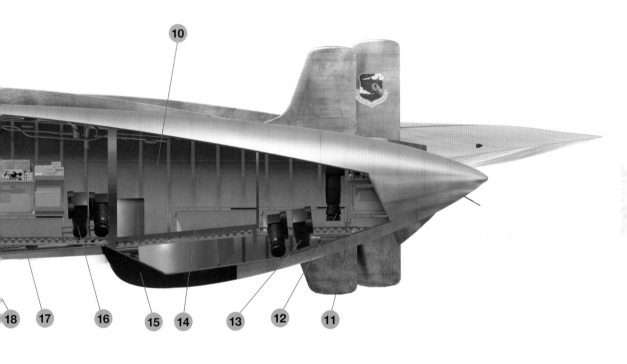

flying wing and was impressed, insisting that Cardenas should fly it at low altitude down Pennsylvania Avenue, Washington, on February 17 and across the Capitol because he "wanted people to see what I'm going to buy." The flight was duly performed at an altitude of 500ft and a speed of 350mph, after which the aircraft proceeded to Wright-Patterson AFB, Ohio.

On return to Muroc, it had to divert urgently to the small airfield at Winslow, Arizona, after fires broke out in four engines, three of them on the left side. Maj Cardenas found that they were caused by oil starvation in the engine bearings, as all eight oil tanks were empty. In another 15 minutes all power would have been lost. It was suspected that there had been inadequate oil replenishment while the YB-49 was at Wright-Patterson, but conspiracy theories (dismissed by Cardenas) about the possibility of sabotage arose and the incident was never resolved. All eight lubricating oil reservoirs had to be refilled whenever the aircraft was refueled, as the system did not re-circulate the oil back to its reservoirs. The flying wing stayed for a month as the star attraction at Winslow airport while new engines were installed, but further damage to its image was inevitable.

At the Northrop Visitors' Day, shortly after the repaired YB-49 had made a nine-hour, 3,000-mile flight, it impressed the onlookers by demonstrating a tighter turning circle and a faster rate of climb than its Lockheed P-80 chase fighter. However, the final blow came during high-speed taxi tests on March 15, 1950 – the day that the flying program had been officially terminated and all remaining B-35 and B-49 contracts had been canceled. Nearing take-off speed at maximum gross weight, the nose wheel shimmied with increasing rapidity on the uneven desert surface and eventually the nose landing gear failed. The YB-49's nose dug into the hardened desert sand and the left wing split off, causing a catastrophic fire. All five crew members including the pilot, Maj Schleeh, and the engineer, MSgt Cunningham, were injured. Ted Coleman commented, "It was almost as if the Air Force was insisting that the flying wing [should] fail."

In the June 1948 crash of the second YB-49, the data from previous USAF test flights was aboard the aircraft and it was destroyed, complicating the investigative process. There was also a lack of knowledge of the precise goals of the fatal test-flight, although stall testing seems to have been a USAF priority. When the YRB-49A tests were flown between May 4 and September 10, 1950, stall testing and recovery procedures had finally been completed. A stall warning light and horn alerted the pilot if the aircraft's speed fell within 13 knots of stalling speed, but advice to avoid the use of rudders in a stall still relied on wind tunnel evidence. (USAF)

FINAL CHANCE – YRB-49A

A conference in April 1948 discussed the USAF's long-delayed decision regarding a strategic reconnaissance aircraft requirement, and Northrop's YB-49 was accepted as a possibility rather than versions

The YRB-49A depicted as a bomber, but in this case the weapon is one of six 188lb T-89 flash bombs that could be carried rather than the typical 16,000lbs of high explosive intended for the YB-49A. Reconnaissance equipment was to be located in five camera stations throughout the central and lower rear areas of the aircraft, with optically flat camera ports covered by doors. (USAF)

of Boeing's B-50 and B-47. However, the latter type was eventually selected, with the much cheaper RB-50A serving as an interim type. Republic entered the four-engined XF-12 Rainbow (still the fastest piston engine aircraft of its size), but 1948 austerity prevented any orders being placed for it. Hughes Aircraft submitted the twin-boom XF-11, which became the subject of a Senate investigation and almost killed Howard Hughes on its first flight.

On March 2, 1948, Northrop had offered an RB-49 with various potential jet engine options, including J40s and General Electric J47s, as used in the B-47. Northrop was authorized, on May 3, 1948, to begin work on an RB-49 version, although serious USAF interest in the B-49 concept had already faded by then. An order for 29 production examples (serials 49-201 to 49-229) was promised on June 12 by Gen Joseph T. McNarney, commander of AMC and later chairman of Convair, with the suggestion that this quantity was "a drop in the bucket" and the final number could well reach 300.

NORTHROP RB-49A "49-220"

NEXT PAGES

The RB-49A seemed, for a while, to be Northrop's best chance of producing Flying Wings in quantity for SAC. In April 1948 it appeared likely that more than 100 would be ordered, with deliveries of three per month after the first batch of 29 (including "49-220") was completed by February 1951. Two podded jet engines increased the internal fuel space for potential long-range photo-reconnaissance missions – probably over Soviet territory at a time when such high-altitude over-flights were still possible. Photo-flash bombs were carried for night-time missions to illuminate targets for the aircraft's five camera stations. Policy changes limited the sole YRB-49A to only 13 test flights between May and September 1950 before the USAF's planned RB-49A Strategic Reconnaissance Wing was abandoned and the aircraft was stored.

The USAF expressed an intention to modernize its Strategic Reconnaissance Groups with five groups of RB-49As (known until March 1951 as FB-49As). LeMay was made aware that most of the Soviet Union was unmapped by aerial photographs, apart from 1941 German reconnaissance of western areas, and the RB-49 seemed to be a way of recouping some of the considerable investment in the bomber. Jack Northrop was relieved that his project was at least receiving a production order.

However, five days later (June 17), the USAF indicated that it regarded the RB-49A mainly as a means of keeping the government-owned Consolidated (Convair) factory going (as a Northrop sub-contractor) when B-36 production ended in 1954. On June 30 Northrop was told that it would produce a few of the aircraft, but the bulk would be manufactured by Consolidated at Fort Worth, Texas. At a meeting of AMC, Northrop, and Convair chiefs on July 16, 1948, attended by Secretary of the Air Force W. Stuart Symington, Jack Northrop was told that, very much against his will, he should actually merge with Convair. The penalties for refusal would be the cancelation of any contracts. In Northrop's opinion, "He did his best, I guess, to wreck the company."

Memories of the failed collaboration with Martin haunted Northrop and increased his frustration at this new attempt to undermine his dream only a few weeks after the loss of the second YB-49. Symington stated bluntly that the USA had too many postwar aircraft companies and one would have to go. Northrop had little doubt about which one he meant. Symington later denied that there was any desire to threaten Northrop and said decisions about the B-49 came entirely from the Air Staff.

Symington, a businessman and future Democratic Senator, was struggling to establish the recently-founded USAF against a background of shrinking defense budgets and opposition from the dominant US Navy. The huge B-36, entering service in 1948, was his centerpiece of that battle. Attacks on its credibility as a weapon resulted in a Congressional hearing claiming fraud in the awarding of the B-36 contract. Symington's defense of the contract was upheld and the bomber's continued production (including reconnaissance versions and a much-revised jet-propelled proposal) until 1953 was assured.

Ted Coleman believed that the fundamental conservatism of USAF generals and the dominant influence of Gen LeMay made them prefer a more conventional aircraft such as the B-36, although they required the YB-49's funding to pay for extra Convair bombers that were needed. There was certainly little room in that debate to support Northrop-manufactured Flying Wings as well as a large B-36 order, which was also a main factor in the cancelation of the US Navy's "supercarrier" USS *United States* (CVA-58).

The arrangement with Convair, owned mainly by Floyd Odlum's Atlas Corporation which had financed Northrop at a difficult time in his career, was seen as a takeover of the Flying Wing and all of Northrop's research, associated companies, and facilities. Odlum, close to Symington, was present at the meeting where the Convair "merger" was proposed, and many regard his influence as the crucial element in the decision. Symington later played down any such connection, claiming that he was merely the bringer of bad news originating from the Air Staff. It was presented to the Northrop workforce as a means of ensuring a production contract, albeit on less than favorable terms, but on the understanding that the company had no space to assemble such massive aircraft in quantity at the USAF's required rate. Even Convair's B-36 assembly line had to be arranged at an awkward diagonal angle because the bomber was wider than its huge main production building.

Meanwhile, the work-rich Fort Worth employees were reluctant to have a Northrop design as successor to their own B-36 even if, as Odlum seemed to imply, it became the Convair RB-49. Knowing that he would have nothing to offer his share-holders, Northrop declined the Convair offer, although he knew it meant the end of substantial flying wing production.

Plans for 30 RB-49As, based on a conversion by Northrop of the surviving YB-49A, were authorized by the USAF's Director of Procurement and Industrial Planning on August 12, 1948, and a contract that day specified that only one RB-49A would be built by Northrop and 29 more at Fort Worth, with Northrop still receiving two-thirds of the profits.

From the 13 YB-35 airframes held still in storage at Hawthorne, 42-102369 was chosen as the YRB-49A. Northrop and AMC discussed the disposition of the rest of the stored B-35 shells, and suggestions included the conversion of nine to jet power with reconnaissance equipment or Turbodyne engines, or even persisting with development of their troubled piston engines. On September 20 it was agreed that one would become the RB-49 prototype, another would test the Turbodyne engines and the rest would be J35-engined YRB-49s. The original 30-aircraft deal was approved on September 18, 1948. At the same time key management roles in the program were transferred to Convair personnel. W. G. Knieriem became Northrop Fort Worth Division Manager on November 16, effectively conferring management of the flying wing on Convair.

That same month the USAF reviewed the project, casting doubts on the RB-49A's range, partly because twin-gun defensive armament had been reintroduced. It foresaw the B-47 in service in 1951, at the same time as the long-delayed, slower early-production RB-49s. Later RB-49B versions with the Northrop Turbodyne engine were considered potentially inferior to the RB-52B Stratofortress, which was due in 1955 – shortly after the fully-developed RB-49B/Turbodyne might be ready. Air Staff representatives, strongly influenced by Gen LeMay at an October 1948 review of SAC's reconnaissance needs, recommended cancelation of the RB-49 on November 12.

This move was reflected in a December 29 meeting of senior officers at which cancelation of seven aircraft projects was decided. The RB-49 was on a list that included 100 Republic F-84s, 51 North American B-45 Tornados, and the F-93 escort fighter, together with the Boeing B-54 "Ultrafortress," an enlarged B-50 bomber. North American orders were particularly badly hit, with a loss of more than $163m

compared with $88.5m for Northrop. The B-36 contract, however, was extended from its original total of 95, and eventually amounted to 384 airframes including reconnaissance versions, funded partly by the many cancelations of other types. Fort Worth later supplied SAC with 116 B-58A Hustler supersonic bombers, followed by 76 swing-wing FB-111As.

Oddly, one of the factors in LeMay's preference for the 435mph B-36 and thin-winged, subsonic B-47 was that the XB-49's thick wing "would not be suitable for supersonic speeds when equipped with jet engines." His views were accepted by Symington (who told Northrop in crude terms that he was canceling the B-49 because he had received "an adverse report" and then hung up, subsequently remaining incommunicado), although Jack Northrop had agreed two years earlier that a thinner wing section could be used to reduce drag further, albeit with a major and extremely costly redesign of the aircraft. In 1947 he also gave convincing reasons why a modified all-wing design could be suitable for high altitude supersonic flight, using "diamond-section aerofoils" rather than the thick, subsonic wing, and accepting reduced internal capacity.

Despite the recommended RB-49 cancelation, work to convert the YB-35s to reconnaissance roles was approved. However, on January 11, 1949 Northrop was finally instructed to stop work on production RB-49s as a jet-assisted RB-36 was to be used instead, pending delivery of RB-47s. Conversion of the YB-35s and the YRB-49A was to continue, and the former would become RB-35B trainers for SAC.

REDESIGNATED SURVIVOR

On January 14, 1949 AMC ordered Northrop to end all RB-49 work, but to continue with the single YRB-49A. Conversion of the YB-35s into RB-35Bs, which would have been used to train crews for the RB-49 Strategic Reconnaissance Wing, continued, despite an

The YRB-49A's two podded engines were necessary as there was insufficient room in the wing-space to house all six of the planned 7,500lb thrust J40 engines, which were larger than the J35. YRB-49A carried the "buzz" number BG-376 alongside its underwing USAF marking, as there was no fuselage to display them in the usual way. A similar marking was applied to YB-35 42-02366 (BG-366). The "BG" "buzz" code was carried over from the canceled Convair B-32 in April 1947. (USAF)

The YB-49's tail cone was meant to be a flexible "stinger" mounting for four 0.50-cal machine guns, but these were removed and not included in the YRB-49A re-design. The rear astrodome could be used as an emergency exit for a "gear-up" landing or an in-flight bail-out in the absence of ejection seats. A crash axe was provided to smash the transparency so the crew could leap out, and four alarm bells warned them of the need to bail out. (Terry Panopalis collection)

increasing sense that the whole project had been overtaken by events, and doubts about the aircraft's lack of precise stability for photographic use.

AMC's uncertainty about the flying wing caused revision of the project in the face of excessive program costs and continued shrinkage in defense funding. Nevertheless, AMC decided to restore two XB-35s and two YB-35s to the program, using a YB-35A as the Turbodyne test-bed (as an EB-35B) instead of the first XB-35. Changes persisted into March 1949, when the abandonment of the RB-49A Reconnaissance Wing plan reduced the specification for the seven RB-35s, due for delivery by May 1950, to jet flight-test vehicles.

The final movement in that confusing saga came in November 1949 when the USAF ordered all seven YB-35Bs to be scrapped, ostensibly to help pay for cost overruns on the whole project. It was unwilling to fund long-term storage of the airframes pending a powerplant solution, which could have cost $25m. Development of the Turbodyne and other gas turbine research was also stopped on Symington's orders and all the Northrop data on that engine was given to General Electric. The sole EB-35B test bed was among the victims of the smelters' blow-torches, leaving only the YRB-49A to represent the Flying Wing program. The USAF made sure to remove all their GFE items, including the engines, before cutting up the shells and making more than 2,000 Northrop employees redundant. No example was retained for a museum and all the production jigs, dies, and engineering drawings were also destroyed, as if to deny the existence of the project. Many USAF reports on the test programs, some of which were allegedly favorable to the YB-49, were also deleted. Similar tactics were used for the Lockheed YF-12A in the USA and the BAC TSR2 in Britain.

As a gesture of loyalty to Northrop and his visionary concept, many of his workers volunteered to complete the last YB-49 in their own time without payment. Jack Northrop was moved by their support, but pointed out that it was a USAF-owned project and their future lay with retaining the good opinion of that customer as a purchaser of their next projects, the F-89 Scorpion fighter and Snark cruise missile. For that reason, he never discussed his dealings with Symington publicly for fear of losing all USAF contracts, and work on the surviving YRB-49A.

To this end, he was obliged to provide a House Committee on Armed Services hearing on August 17, 1949 with a favorable account of the USAF's treatment of Northrop over the selection of the B-36, denying that there had been political coercion from Secretary Symington or unfairness in the transfer of RB-49 manufacturing to

Fort Worth. Despite his obligatory acquiescence in the USAF's political maneuvering, two days later the B-35 shells were destroyed.

Northrop had to accept that his revolutionary concept was portrayed as inferior to the very conventional B-36, a bomber whose engines routinely caught fire and which, until its undercarriage was redesigned, could only operate from two bases because its nine-foot-wide main wheels would break through normal runways. The revelation of the XB-49's stealth characteristics also contrasted strongly with the large and distinctive image that a slow-moving B-36 would provide for Soviet radars, but LeMay was convinced that the massive Convair bomber would still get through by flying above the defenses. Within a few years Soviet ground-to-air missiles would render that idea totally impractical.

On May 4, 1950 the final revision of Jack Northrop's B-35 concept, now re-imagined as the N-41/YRB-49A (42-102376), finally took to the air with Fred C. Bretcher at the controls. He was joined by co-pilot Dale Johnson and flight engineer Frank Schroeder. It had completed only 18 hours of tests by September 10, 1950, evaluating overall stability, yaw stabilization, and weapons delivery using flare bombs. Its revised tandem cockpit complied with USAF requirements. Power was provided by six Allison J35-A-19 engines, although alternative studies used eight General Electric J47s or six Westinghouse J40s. Four were in the wing, with two in the nacelles suspended on pylons beneath it, adding some directional stability and allowing more internal space for 12 fuel tanks, but increasing drag.

A radio operator/photo-navigator's position with a camera control panel and a B-2 photo viewfinder was set up in the co-pilot's area behind the pilot. Photo-flash bombs could be carried in two of the bomb-bays, but no bombardier was required and the navigator became a radar navigator in charge of the AN/APQ-24 bombing/navigation equipment. In keeping with standard SAC crew comfort, two electrically-heated hot cups were located in the central crew nacelle for the essential supplies of coffee.

All of its 13 flights, totaling only 17 hours and 40 minutes, were relatively uneventful apart from the August 10 sortie. The pilots' canopy had been made jettisonable at the USAF's request, and it blew off at 35,000ft and 225mph. Luckily, the crew suffered no serious harm from the depressurization, because the pilot was given emergency oxygen after his own mask was lost in the airstream.

Stations for cameras in the tail remained empty of equipment. The definitive YB-49 (N-40) was also meant to have a Minneapolis Honeywell E-7 autopilot, gun turrets and, like the YRB-49A, an AN/APQ-24 bombing/navigation radar set in a fairing beneath the rear fuselage. At the end of the tests the YRB-49 made its only flight by a USAF crew when Col Albert Boyd took it back to Northrop's Ontario Airport base on April 26, 1951, at Jack Northrop's request, where he still hoped that it could have been equipped at last with its Minneapolis Honeywell autopilot. It was stored there in the open for more than two years until November 17, 1953, when it became the last Flying Wing to be scrapped a year after Jack Northrop finally abandoned his hopes for the project.

CHAPTER FIVE

WHAT MIGHT HAVE BEEN

The line-up of uncompleted Flying Wings, seen in December 1948 as the end of Jack Northrop's dream approached. Two XB-35s and two YB-35s were salvaged in July 1949, but the rest had been turned into metal ingots by March 30, 1950 – five weeks before the first flight of the sole YRB-49A, which survived until December 1, 1953. Jack Northrop had left the aircraft industry a month earlier. (Terry Panopalis collection)

Jack Northrop's frustration as his vision of future flight was increasingly clouded by politicians and their industrial allies, military chiefs and disappointing sub-contractors eventually drove him out of his own company in November 1952, aged 57. In 1950 he could still conjecture alternatives to the military flying wing and the company continued to pursue civilian versions of the YB-49, to be met with total indifference by the airlines, which were unwilling to risk investment in such radical concepts.

A glamorous Hollywood film was made to promote the idea of a 50- to 80-seat luxury airliner from which passengers could view the landscape through leading-edge windows and from an observation blister in the tail, while sipping cocktails or enjoying gourmet meals in a more spacious environment than other airliners could offer. Jack Northrop circumvented the lack of sideways visibility by claiming that "the really interesting views are likely to be forward and downward rather than to the side." He patented designs for civilian "all-wing" aircraft with either two Turbodyne or four turbojet engines in April 1949. Both had tandem seating for the pilots. He preferred to think of his designs as potential peace-time passenger transports, but World War II and the Cold War demanded military applications, and the all-wing airliner duly remained a fantasy.

The immediate postwar reduction in aircraft production allowed Northrop a small order for 24 company-designed YC-125A/B high-wing tri-motor transports, but the company was also obliged to take on routine job-creation activities such as reconditioning C-47 transport aircraft for civilian use, while other companies were designing new airliners.

The flying wing bomber idea persisted into 1950 as Jack Northrop reacted to the USAF's criticisms of the B-49's stability problems, but it was never supplied with a suitable auto-stabilization or auto-pilot system to remedy them. He also realized that the need for a massive bomb-bay for thermonuclear weapons required an extensive re-design of the basic Flying Wing that would place the tandem crew cabin in an extended nose and allow a large space in the center of the wing for weapons. Wingspan was reduced to 128ft 4in. and power came from two Northrop Turbodyne V engines developing a total of 20,000hp and driving six-bladed contra-rotating propellers.

Jack Northrop's last flying wing or tailless project before resigning from his company was the N-69/SM-62 Snark missile, which was developed and tested over a period of ten years. Two long skids extended below the fuselage for recovery on a landing field, although many early N-69A/Bs ended up in the sea instead. Snark was canceled in 1951 in favor of the North American Navaho missile. (Terry Panopalis collection)

The tail extension was similar to the XB-49's, and would have housed up to four remotely-controlled 0.50-cal machine guns. Two other crew-members occupied positions in the wing's leading edge, with good forward visibility, while the flight engineer had his instrument panels in the rear of the cabin. The estimated performance was impressive, with a cruising speed of 517mph and a range of 5,580 miles with the newly-introduced benefit of in-flight refueling. It could weigh up to 161,540lbs on the ground, increasing to 222,710lbs after an in-flight refueling session.

Northrop also proposed a turbojet version of the Turbodyne and another with very short supersonic propeller blades. Two Turbodynes were also intended for one of the N-31 series of bombers, reconnaissance and transport adaptations of the B-49, using the 128ft wingspan and various engine combinations – one had four buried turbojets and two mounted on the wingtips. Escort fighter/interceptor variants with a projecting nose section containing air-to-air radar equipment would have loitered with a load of 44 AIM-4 guided missiles firing fore and aft to intercept an incoming bomber stream. Another spin-off proposal to rival the B-36 was the "Turbo Wing" with four Allison turboprops and two under-slung jets for take-off, offering a 12,000-mile range at 459mph, while the N-55 was a Turbodyne-powered, long-range patrol and radar picket aircraft. Northrop also outlined a transport version with four Allison T40 turboprops, each offering 7,500hp in a similar airframe.

SNARKS AND SCORPIONS

Breaking new ground, Northrop won a development contract for an early ground-launched, 600mph cruise missile with a 2,000lb warhead – the subsonic N-25A/XSSM-A-3 Snark. The J33 jet-powered 52ft-long pilotless missile attracted Northrop partly because it provided another extension of the tailless flight idea, with elevons on the wings. The company developed a successful daylight star-tracking system for the missile's journey of up to 5,000 miles.

Canceled in 1946 but reinstated by Northrop's efforts the following year, it made encouraging test flights but ever-changing USAF requirements meant it had to be redesigned as the 69ft-long N-69/SM-62 Snark intercontinental ballistic missile with a J57 engine, rocket-boosted zero-length take-off, and a W39 nuclear weapon in a jettisonable nose section. The rest of the airframe would fly back to base after an 11,000-mile journey. Limited numbers entered service in 1959, and they were replaced within two years by ballistic missiles.

The original N-25A Snark successor on the drawing board in 1946 was the supersonic 51ft-long N-25B/XSSM-A-5 Boojum (like "Snark," a Lewis Carroll name) with a large delta wing, a small central fuselage, and two podded, afterburning J35 or J47 turbojets on its wingtips.

Both missile projects faced extreme difficulty in meeting the challenging long-range, pilotless guidance criteria at a time when light-weight computers were in their infancy. Northrop engineers, managed by Eldon Weaver, had to build their own (known as the Magnetic Drum Differential Analyzer) and work with existing maps, which were sometimes found to be quite inaccurate. When the computer team, sensing development prospects in that field, asked to form the Northrop Electronic Computer Division, Jack turned down their proposal and stuck to his belief that the company should focus on aircraft. Many of them left and set up highly-profitable computer companies, originating ideas for IBM and the next generation of military aircraft that would rely on digital technology.

There were also projects in the 1940s based on developed versions of the XP-79 tailless fighter that took the company towards the early stages of the Century Series of fighter-bombers. As a long-range "penetration" or SAC escort fighter, with an alternative rocket-powered interceptor version, Northrop's swept-wing, tailless XP-79Z Skylancer was in at the beginning of a series of US fighter projects that eventually led to the Lockheed XF-93 and McDonnell F-101 Voodoo.

Ironically, his success in this area came from a fairly conventional submission for an all-weather interceptor requirement which appears to have originated from the XP-79Z. The twin-jet N-24/F-89 Scorpion, a replacement for the P-61 Black Widow, began as a swept-wing, triple-jet design with a chubby fuselage derived from XP-56 ideas and containing a substantial magnesium structure. By September 1946 it had a thin straight aluminum wing, a high-mounted conventional empennage, and two turbojets. An innovative, swiveling, four-gun nose turret was later replaced by free-flight rocket armament. It was Northrop's last design for his company, but one which kept it alive after his departure with orders for 1,052 aircraft. Although it was persistently underpowered, the interceptor entered production in 1949 and served for ten years, with a final F-89J version carrying Genie nuclear rockets and AIM-4 Falcon guided missiles.

FLYING BANTAM

Although there was a postwar decline in military aircraft orders, significant funds were devoted to the creation of experimental aircraft, dubbed "X-planes." The war had generated very adventurous research for high-speed flight, but little time to prove many of those radical designs and theories in the air. Lacking modern computer simulation, for manufacturers the only solution was to build pure research prototypes and allow intrepid test pilots to take them to their limits.

Bell's rocket-powered X-1 and X-2, with the Douglas D-558, had taken maximum speeds to Mach 1, then Mach 2, and explored controllability at high altitude and high Mach numbers, where searing temperatures required completely new approaches to airframe construction. The Douglas X-3 Stiletto, with tiny wings and a slender, pointed low-drag fuselage almost 67ft in length was also intended to explore the use of jet engines for more sustained Mach 2 endurance. It was impossible to find suitably-powerful turbojets at the time, and the X-3 first flew in 1952, demonstrating a take-off speed of 260mph, extremely difficult handling characteristics, and a severe lack of power, which limited the speed of this impressively-futuristic design to Mach 1.21 in a dive. On several of its 54 flights it did reveal the potentially-fatal problem known as inertia coupling, which would cause an aircraft to lose control completely, sometimes with fatal results.

The twin-jet N-24/F-89 Scorpion was acquired by the USAF as a replacement for the P-61 Black Widow. Jack Northrop's last design for his company, and one that kept it alive after his departure with orders for 1,052 aircraft, the Scorpion was persistently underpowered. The F-89 entered production in 1949 and served for ten years, these particular examples being J-models of Air Defense Command's 59th Fighter Interceptor Squadron based at Goose Bay, Canada, in the late 1950s. (USAF)

Technicians work on the X-4 at Edwards AFB in November 1948. Unlike several early X-planes, the X-4 had an ejection seat and good visibility from the cockpit. The aircraft had a series of red bands painted all over it for early tests. The X-4s were retired in September 1953, having proved that until better auto-stabilization systems were available, the tailless configuration was unsuitable for supersonic or high transonic speeds. Both examples survived and were finally displayed at the USAF Academy (46-676) and the USAF Museum in Dayton, Ohio (46-677). (USAF)

Northrop constructed the next in the X-plane series, and it extended aspects of the flying wing idea to one of the smallest jet aircraft ever built, although the N-26 X-4 Bantam had a conventional fuselage and vertical tail. It was initially proposed in 1946 as an amalgam of Northrop's interest in flying wings and the USAAF's knowledge of the Me 163 tailless rocket fighter, after captured examples were examined. It owed much to the XP-79 series of designs, and its long-term purpose was to study the behavior of airflow over the wing during transonic flight. The resulting Project MX-810, or Project *Skylancer*, attracted a contract for two swept-wing prototypes.

Like de Havilland in Britain with the similar DH 108, Northrop's team, led by Arthur Lusk, opted for jet power rather than a rocket motor. The X-4s had split wingtip flap airbrake installations placed inboard and elevon controls like other Northrop flying wings. Two Westinghouse XJ30 turbojets, used in the XP-79, provided a total of 3,200lbs of thrust. This was adequate for lively performance from the tiny X-4 with a wingspan of 29ft 9in., weighing only 5,500lbs when empty.

The two white X-4s, 46-676 and 46-677, were built while Northrop continued to work on the XP-79B. He used a similar magnesium skin for the X-4 wing, but abandoned the prone pilot position and provided a fighter-type bubble canopy. The first aircraft was flown by Charles Tucker on December 16, 1948, and persistent mechanical problems, oil leaks, and excessive maintenance on the early, temperamental jet engines limited it to only ten flights before it had to be cannibalized to keep 46-677 active. Northrop and USAF pilots flew it on 20 occasions, finding that the X-4 tended to pitch up sharply at transonic speeds. A further 82 flights were made under the auspices of NACA after its instrumentation had been squeezed into the second aircraft in place of some extra fuel tank space. Spin recovery parachutes were installed.

Among the early USAF pilots to fly the X-4 was Capt Chuck Yeager, who was impressed by the way the aircraft's large airbrakes held its speed to 250mph in a near-vertical dive, as well as their proficiency in rapidly-decelerating the jet if it approached dangerous instability at speed. However, when he reached Mach 0.92 the little aircraft became increasingly unstable and began to porpoise rapidly and then spin violently. Conscious of parallels with the DH 108, which had broken up and killed Geoffrey de Havilland after pitching uncontrollably at Mach 0.875, Yeager's team "quit right there and junked her." For him, transonic aircraft needed tails. He had one more encounter with the X-4 when flying chase for NACA pilot Joe Walker, whose oxygen system failed, causing the rapid onset of hypoxia. Yeager talked the semi-conscious Walker down to a safe landing and the X-4 survived.

Test pilot Scott Crossfield also flew the X-4 for NACA, and was told that its engines flamed out at altitude. When he attempted a loop at 27,000ft he experienced this situation as his maneuver disrupted the airflow into the engine inlets. He only managed a partial re-start of one engine before bringing the X-4 in for an emergency landing. Crossfield did fly higher in the aircraft, achieving in excess of 42,000ft on one occasion. The porpoising phenomenon was partially overcome by thickening the wings' trailing edge with wooden spacer blocks to keep the flaps slightly open. A similar effect was achieved for Bell's X-2 by making the trailing edges noticeably blunt.

Some of the X-4 and XP-79 flying control ideas were reflected in the F-89 Scorpion, including the split ailerons that doubled as airbrakes or "decelerons." When early F-89Cs suffered a series of wing attachment fatigue failures at a time when such problems were not well understood, Jack Northrop immediately set about devising a solution. However, the new Northrop chairman, Oliver Echols, brought in another engineer (Ed Schmued) over Jack's head to work on the problem and implied that Schmued would take over as chief engineer in his place. Jack, who was used to having control of engineering and personnel matters, disagreed strongly and resigned. His legacy was one of visionary, original design skill rather than hard-headed business sense.

After Northrop's departure, the management resisted innovative ideas, and much of the research data and engineering drawing archive for the Flying Wing projects were destroyed under Schmued's management, while Jack Northrop's name and reputation were effectively erased in an attempt to reinvent Northrop as a corporate supplier to the USAF. With his retirement, flying wing development stopped until the late 1970s.

A new regime took over from chairman Whitney Collins and Ed Schmued in the mid-1950s, and under accomplished engineer Thomas V. Jones the company revived and produced the T-38 Talon trainer and F-5 Freedom Fighter, which won large domestic and export contracts, respectively, while Jack Northrop's interests in semi-retirement turned to establishing the Northrop Aeronautical Institute, renamed Northrop University in 1975. He also pursued business interests in pre-fabricated housing in the 1960s, but lost considerable sums in a housing deal that went wrong. It was the last of many unfortunate business outcomes in his career, but he was at least rewarded by his old company with the role of Director Emeritus, which gave him a modest income to compensate for his loss. He died in 1981 after finally breaking his silence about his treatment by Stuart Symington and the cancelation of the Flying Wing bombers.

CHAPTER SIX

THE SPIRIT LIVES ON

Although arguably more like a flying fuselage than a flying wing, the M2-F1 showed in towed and glide flight in 1963 that the idea behind it could form the basis of a re-entry vehicle for space research. Flown from Edwards AFB by X-15 pilot Milt Thompson, and also by Chuck Yeager, Don Mallick, and Bruce Peterson from the X-planes programs, it was initially tow-launched like Northrop's earlier MX-334 glider. The M2-F1 was later air-towed by a C-47, reaching 150mph in a steep descent and proving that lifting bodies could land safely after re-entry from high altitude. (NASA)

Under the leadership of Thomas V. Jones, Northrop Corporation became a large, multi-national organization, substantially free of government subsidy and control and able to venture into a wide range of innovative advanced technologies including electronics, communications, and navigation systems. A deal with former partner Boeing risked a large proportion of Northrop's corporate wealth in taking on the detailed design and manufacture of Boeing 747 fuselage sections from 1966.

A less profitable arrangement gave Northrop a share of the Boeing 2707 supersonic transport design work until that project was canceled. However, the company became a major innovator in the field of lifting body test vehicles, which led to the Space Shuttle. The M2-F1 (first flown in 1963), designed and built by the National Aeronautics and Space Administration (NASA) and the Briegleb Glider Company, used Northrop's familiar steel tube and plywood skin construction, but it was in some ways the antithesis of the flying wing, being more like a 20ft-long bathtub-shaped flying fuselage.

In 1966 Northrop developed the M2-F1 into the much heavier M2-F2, launched from a B-52 and flown by several NASA pilots including Milt Thompson of X-15 fame. Despite an auto-stabilization system, its lack of conventional lifting surfaces made roll control difficult, and Bruce Peterson experienced pilot-induced oscillations that ended in a crash-landing at Edwards AFB in 1967. Re-built as the M2-F3, with an additional vertical stabilizer, it was flown by X-15 pilot Bill Dana to 66,300ft and Mach 1.3 in 1972 and went on to reach Mach 1.6 and 71,500ft later that year. The M2-F3 pioneered

the reaction control thrusters used on spacecraft and side-arm flying control "sticks" later installed in many other aircraft.

A parallel Northrop design effort produced the HL-10 with a delta wing and a curious, curved, "inverted aerofoil" body profile. Like the M2-F3, it used the trusty XLR-11 rocket motor employed in the X-1 and early X-15 flights. Launched from a B-52B, it exceeded 90,000ft and Mach 1.86 on one of its 37 flights, and there were proposals to make it Northrop's first manned orbital spacecraft.

The company's successful F-5/T-38 and N-102 Fang fighter series evolved into the N-300, or YF-17A Cobra, for the USAF's Lightweight Fighter competition in 1971. Although it lost to the F-16 in another battle with Convair, by then a division of General Dynamics, the YF-17A was developed as a joint venture with McDonnell Douglas and eventually became the F/A-18 Hornet, mainstay of the US Navy and several air forces. Northrop's F-20 Tigershark freelance project was a further but sadly unsuccessful development of the F-5 that offered some advantages in cost and practicality over the F-16. Not ordered or encouraged by the USAF, it found no other customers as a result and lost Northrop $1.2bn. The company's credibility was also severely damaged.

In 1986 Northrop and McDonnell Douglas were selected to compete with a Lockheed, Boeing, and General Dynamics consortium for the USAF's Advanced Tactical Fighter. Northrop's YF-23A Black Widow II, named as a tribute to Jack Northrop, used advanced stealth structural techniques and had two "buried" 35,000lb thrust turbofans. The first aircraft flew on June 22, 1990 and demonstrated impressive performance, but the USAF decision favored the very similar rival bid, which became the F-22 Raptor in 1991. Northrop's heavy involvement in work on a new bomber and the N-370/AGM-137A stealthy cruise missile (canceled in 1994 after eight years of costly research) were political factors that came in to play when choosing the Lockheed fighter.

Northrop's N-345 *Tacit Blue* technology demonstrator pioneered "stealth" characteristics in a surveillance aircraft. It was funded for three years of secret tests within the USAF's *Pave Mover* radar program, which examined the use of air power to counter large-scale enemy armored vehicle attacks. N-345 relied entirely on digital fly-by-wire controls to overcome its inherent instability, the aircraft's success proving that the company had enough expertise to continue as a separate entity as Jack Northrop would have hoped, rather than entering a planned merger with Lockheed Martin in 1998. (USAF)

Several "black" secret projects (under a selection and funding competition code-named *Aurora*) followed the *Have Blue* program that studied stealth aircraft characteristics and led to the AGM-137A and the Lockheed Martin F-117 attack aircraft. In 1974 the Defense Advanced Research Projects Agency (DARPA) asked companies to research the reduction of radar cross-section (RCS) as a means of survival for aircraft in a high-threat environment. Interestingly, Convair (General Dynamics) declined, stating that it did not believe that reduced RCS, or "stealth," would have significant effects unless it was paired with active electronic countermeasures (ECM) – not the purpose of DARPA's request.

Northrop and McDonnell Douglas pursued study contracts with the aim of reducing RCS by a factor of 10,000. Lockheed asked to be included based on its RCS reduction work on the U-2 spyplane and A-12 "Blackbird." Their solution (using long-established and published Soviet research) for the F-117A involved an airframe made up from a series of flat panels or facets to reflect radar energy. The resulting "bevelled diamond" structure offered very low RCS but limited flight characteristics.

Northrop's approach was based on a computer program called GENSCAT, which could determine the RCS of curved surfaces. Although Lockheed's F-117A was selected for production, Northrop was asked to produce a low-observable Battlefield Surveillance Aircraft, Experimental (BSAX) that led to the bathtub-shaped N-345 *Tacit Blue* manned stealth surveillance aircraft, nicknamed "the whale." A well-preserved secret until 1996, its combination of curves and rectangular edges, with hidden intakes for its ATF3-6 engines, made the BSAX virtually invisible even to low-frequency radars. It flew 135 times from 1982 to 1985, yielding valuable data on low observability that would assist Northrop with its next major project, the Advanced Technology Bomber (ATB).

BACK TO BOMBERS

Northrop's lifting bodies proved that wings were not vital components in an aircraft, but it was the ATB program, begun in 1979, that took Northrop back into flying wings and the bomber business 30 years after the cancelation of the B-49. When the company received the request to adapt its low observability knowledge to a large strategic bomber, CEO Thomas V. Jones, advised that he should bid, promised a response within six weeks. Designers John Cashen and Irv Waaland decided to aim for a high-altitude, subsonic design in a project named *Senior Ice* (later, *Senior Cejay*) directed by Hal Markarian.

The quest for a supersonic heavy bomber had died with the cancelation of the North American XB-70 Valkyrie and Rockwell B-1A, opening up more possibilities for innovative subsonic designs. They started with "a clean sheet of paper" according to Waaland, examining all options and even looking over the preserved Horten Ho IX flying wing, although their ideas were based far more upon original calculations to ensure a very small RCS. Large aircraft operating undetected at night over hostile territory had freedom of movement compared with

bombers that followed set routes. They could also survive without many of the complex ECM defenses that occupy considerable space in a B-52 or B-1B.

Designers quickly saw the benefits of a flying wing for low RCS, reviving thoughts of Jack Northrop's XB-49 and the discovery of its fortuitously low radar signature. Lockheed eventually drew similar conclusions for its rival bid. Max Stanley was involved in early simulator trials for the B-2, and he commented that it flew just like the B-49, although the final B-2A design resulted in a very different aircraft. The initial ATB design used a diamond-shaped center section with swept, outboard wing sections that took the span to 172ft (the same as the XB-49 – a coincidence according to the design team) and gave excellent lift/drag and transonic aerodynamic characteristics.

ATB initially had vertical stabilizers or small reaction jets on the wingtips, but they were discarded in favor of B-49-type split flaps as rudders. Although the designers faced similar stability issues to the flying wing pioneers of the 1940s, tremendous advances in computerized, digital auto-stabilization meant that they could make an aircraft that was inherently unstable in both pitch and yaw axes fly with unprecedented stability (for a flying wing) due to its Digital Flight Control System (DFCS). Power came from four non-afterburning General Electric F101-GE-F29 turbofans, with intakes above the center body. Although its W-shaped trailing edge differed from the XB-49's, there were some similarities, not least in the landing gear arrangement and position of the (much larger) weapons bay.

While meaningful comparisons are difficult, it is of interest that the B-2A's basic range is more than 2,000 miles greater than the YB-49's 4,000 miles, and this can be increased to 11,500 miles with one in-flight refueling – close to the USAAF's original 1941 requirement for the B-35 or B-36. Its combined engine thrust of 69,200lbs, more than twice the power of the YB-49, allows a maximum take-off weight of 376,000lbs, compared with 194,000lbs for the YB-49, although maximum speed is only around 50mph faster. (USAF)

In the Northrop tradition, the designers used new metals – in this case titanium alloys and composites, including elastomeric coating for the exterior. The USAF was expected to order 132 ATBs, with a service entry date of 1987. Construction was to be shared between Northrop (the nose, cockpit, wing leading and trailing edges, and flying controls, including three-part elevons on each wing) and Boeing which, with Vought, produced the rest.

In April 1980 Jack Northrop, who had been out of contact with his company since he left it in November 1952, was brought back to Hawthorne to be shown some of the secret work on the new bomber. Aged 85 and suffering from Parkinson's disease, he stood and carefully examined a model of the ATB, commenting, "Now I know why God has kept me alive so long." He had already received endorsement for his ideas after a meeting with NASA aeronautical researchers in 1976, at which the use of a flying wing for effective span loading (distributing payloads evenly across an airframe) was discussed in relation to NASA's future visions of large commercial aircraft.

Robert Frosch, NASA Administrator, wrote to Jack saying that in the course of their research they had, "in effect, rediscovered the flying wing. Obviously we recognize the pioneering Northrop work in that area as an essential source of information, and in the course of our investigations we re-examined considerable NASA B-35/YB-49 wind tunnel data. Our analyses confirmed your much earlier conviction as to the load-carrying and efficiency advantages of this design approach, and studies performed for us by the major manufacturers of large aeroplanes have further corroborated these findings."

Boeing's 250ft span, flying wing "Spanloader" project was one outcome of this reaffirmation of Northrop's 1940s research. Other projects envisaged flying wing derivatives spanning 500ft and weighing up to five million pounds. These ambitious concepts were still in keeping with Jack Northrop's assertion at his 1947 Wilbur Wright Memorial Lecture that one of the basic requirements for a flying wing is that "the airplane must be large enough so that the all-wing principle can be fully utilized. This is a matter closely related to the density of the elements comprising the empty weight and the useful load to be carried within the wing."

Northrop was asked to offer a fully-worked ATB proposal, which was rivaled by stealth expert Lockheed's *Senior Peg* proposal in association with Rockwell International. Rockwell, with B-1B stealth experience in its favor, also lobbied for a second batch of 100 B-1Bs as a quicker bomber solution than waiting for the untried B-2. However, Northrop partnered with Boeing and Vought and won the competition in October 1981. Since the time of the B-35 and B-49, bombing had moved from high altitude to become an "under-the-radar at 200ft penetration task at high subsonic speed". This requirement caused far-reaching design changes as work progressed in secrecy, and led to a decision to modify the high-altitude ATB and rename it B-2A rather than start a new design.

Canceled contracts and shrinkage in defense funding following the apparent end of the Cold War in 1991 had drastic effects on the B-2 program, which had already incurred more than $2bn in extra costs to adapt it for low-altitude penetration. The airframe had to be reinforced to withstand the new demands and the wing was extended rearwards into its distinctive saw-tooth profile, providing larger flying control areas and improved gust resistance. Three-part elevons were used on either side, rather than the single versions on the B-49. Mishaps such as the June 1948 YB-49 crash were prevented by a DFCS that stops the aircraft from entering unfavorable AoA or potential stall situations, while four computers work together to ensure stable flight. The aircraft has the same wingspan as the XB-35 and almost the same height, but its 35 degrees wing-sweep gave it another 13ft of length. Rather than the nine crew of the B-35, it was operated by two, with an option for a third crew member.

Its quadruplex, computerized fly-by-wire controls finally solved the flying wing's inherent instability problems in ways which were unimagined by the designers of the B-35. Like the B-49, the B-2 flies with its wingtip rudders slightly open most of the time. Its leading-edge sweepback is very similar to the B-52's, and only slightly greater than the XB-49's. Savings were made where possible – for example, the main landing gear was adapted from Boeing's 767 airliner.

Considerable work was needed to devise appropriate radar-absorbing materials and airframe coatings to defeat low-frequency enemy radars and produce an RCS of less than 0.5sq ft. Allegedly 90 percent of the aircraft's radar invisibility derives from its stealthy flying wing shape, with the engines and their exhausts above the airframe. This work continued after the first aircraft flew on July 17, 1989, some two years later than first projected and a few months after delivery of the final B-1B. In the early 1990s, when cost figures became known, the need for such a sophisticated weapon was questioned and cancelation became a real threat as the USAF struggled to keep its hugely expensive F-22 Raptor program alive too. Instead, the original requirement for 132 aircraft was reduced to 75 and, finally, to 21, resulting in huge unit costs of at least $2bn per aircraft. This in turn made the loss of a B-2A flying from Andersen AFB in February 2008 a major catastrophe. Operating in Guam's notoriously humid conditions, it was affected by moisture on three of its air pressure sensors, causing false information to reach the computers and resulting in an unrecoverable stall on take-off.

The first operational B-2A was delivered to the 509th Bomb Wing at Whiteman AFB, Missouri, in December 1993, and the aircraft made its combat debut over Serbia in March 1999 during Operation *Allied Force*. Many subsequent missions have been flown over Afghanistan, Libya, and Iraq from bases in the USA and Diego Garcia, with at least one lasting for 50 hours.

The B-2A Spirit has highly sophisticated operational equipment that was unimaginable in the B-35 era. In addition to its DFCS, the aircraft has a Raytheon AN/APQ-181 J-band strike radar that provides terrain following and allows covert use for bombing. It has unjammable satellite connection capability, digital engine control systems, and Link 16 to transmit and receive data from other aircraft. Its ability

A USAF-released artist's concept of what the Long-Range Strike-Bomber (unveiled in 2016), known as the B-21 Raider, could look like. Developed by Northrop Grumman under a 2015 contract, and utilizing "stealth" technology gained from unmanned aircraft projects, quantity production of up to 200 units is envisaged so that the B-21 can replace USAF Global Strike Command's "Legacy Bombers" – the B-1B Lancer and, finally, the B-52H – from 2030. The B-21 is due to commence operational service from 2025, and initial contracts were authorized by President Donald Trump in 2017. (USAF)

to carry a wide range of smart weapons, as well as nuclear stores, in much larger weapons bays than the YB-49's makes it a versatile attacker that can strike over four separate targets on a mission lasting for up to 30 hours.

Although the B-2A is a formidable weapon and still unmatched by any other nation, its small production numbers prompted several suggestions for developed versions. Among them was the multi-sensor RB-2A, which contained echoes of the 1950 YRB-49A project, and the EB-2A signals intelligence variant (SIGINT) – a virtually unknown concept in the 1950s. In 2001 Northrop Grumman also proposed re-opening production for a batch of 40 B-2Cs, prioritized for conventional weapons and featuring other unspecified improvements. Although there was support from President George W. Bush's administration, political opposition ensured that no further B-2s were manufactured.

Instead, a new program, the Long-Range Strike-Bomber, was unveiled in 2016, leading to the design of the B-21 Raider. Developed by Northrop Grumman under a 2015 contract, and utilizing "stealth" technology gained from unmanned aircraft projects, such as the X-47A Pegasus demonstrator, the provisional images of the aircraft bore a strong resemblance to the ATB in outline. Quantity production of up to 200 units was envisaged so that the B-21 could replace USAF Global Strike Command's "Legacy Bombers" – the B-1B Lancer and, finally, the B-52H – from 2030.

Continuing Northrop's long tradition of versatility in using the flying wing concept, it is likely that the B-21 will operate as a battlefield management platform, SIGINT vehicle, and even as a missile-launching interceptor. Although Northrop planned to invest in more advanced radar-absorbent coatings, the Raider may well have its own Penetrating Counter-Air escort fighter for missions into high-threat areas – another echo of 1940s-thinking when SAC experimented with long-range escort fighters like the F-101A Voodoo to protect the B-36. The B-21 is due to commence operational service from 2025, and initial contracts were authorized by President Donald Trump in 2017.

In most of the modern century flying wings, manned and unmanned, Jack Northrop's basic concept has tended to evolve into a "blended-wing-body" (BWB) configuration, with engine intakes and exhaust above the aircraft to increase its stealth capabilities. Originating in Junkers' 1910 passenger-carrying flying wings, and Vincent Burnelli's work on lifting body flying wings in the 1920s, the BWB idea was developed in the 1980s by McDonnell Douglas to combine the lifting properties of an aerofoil-shaped body, offering greater internal space than a simple all-wing design, with the high lift, weight-saving, and low drag properties of the flying wing. Boeing/McDonnell Douglas and Lockheed Martin invested in studies for large passenger-carrying BWB aircraft that would also have military applications as tankers, surveillance platforms, and long-range transports. Jack Northrop's dream of a luxurious flying wing airliner might therefore still be realized, albeit almost a century after he first suggested it.

The Northrop-led consortium worked on a smaller version of the ATB for the US Navy's Advanced Tactical Aircraft (ATA) as successor to the Grumman A-6 Intruder in the 1980s. Spanning 80ft, the two-seater aircraft's all-wing planform resembled the ATB. It was to be powered by two General Electric F404 non-afterburning turbofans. As costs became unrealistic Northrop effectively stepped aside and the contract went instead to the McDonnell Douglas and General Dynamics bid in January 1988. The resulting A-12 Avenger II encountered disastrous cost overruns and technical problems that prompted its cancelation in 1991.

Northrop submitted another US Navy flying wing proposal in the mid-1980s. The N-381 Manta was a twin-turbofan aircraft with a stubby fuselage and either one or two vertical tails that could have performed an anti-submarine warfare role, acted as an ECM platform, or undertaken carrier onboard delivery roles, as well as carrying air-to-air missiles for self-defense. Lack of funding left the idea on the drawing board.

Even more radical flying wing designs emerged from the Northrop design offices following studies of oblique flying wing (OFW) aircraft by NASA in the 1970s. Using another World War II German idea originated at Blohm & Voss by Dr Richard Vogt, the design used the qualities of variable-sweep wings to adapt to both high and low speeds without the weighty mechanism associated with a "swing wing."

In 2006 DARPA awarded Northrop Grumman a contract to explore OFW, and several designs appeared, some with pivoting nacelles under a wing optimized for supersonic flight. Another stealth bomber variant had engines buried in a swiveling center-section area of an oblique wing. No doubt Jack Northrop would have explored this unusual concept, possibly making it a practical option. However, as with so many of his initiatives, it was curtailed by lack of funds. He would no doubt have been relieved, though, to know that his efforts have so far resulted in the most successful applications of the flying wing idea, and that they have led to many other evolutions that will probably take it well into the next century.

FURTHER READING

BOOKS

Chong, Tony, *Flying Wings and Radical Things: Northrop's Secret Aerospace Projects & Concepts 1939–1994* (Specialty Press, Forest Lake, MN, 2016)

Coleman, Ted, *Jack Northrop and the Flying Wing: The Real Story Behind the Stealth Bomber* (Paragon House, New York, NY, 1988)

Darling, Kev, *American X & Y Planes – Vol. II, Experimental Aircraft Since 1945* (Crowood Press, Ramsbury, Wiltshire, 2010)

Ford, Daniel, *Glen Edwards – The Diary of a Bomber Pilot* (Smithsonian Books, Washington, DC, 1998)

Gunston, Bill, *Northrop's Flying Wings: Wings of Fame Vol. 2* (Aerospace Publishing, London, 1996)

Holder, Bill, *Northrop Grumman B-2 Spirit: An Illustrated History* (Schiffer Military History, Atglen, PA, 1998)

Jenkins, Dennis R., *Magnesium Overcast: the Story of the Convair B-36* (Specialty Press, North Branch, MN, 2001)

Kozak, Warren, *LeMay: the Life and Wars of General Curtis LeMay* (Regnery History, Washington, DC, 2011)

Pape, Garry R. and Campbell, John M., *Northrop Flying Wings: A History of Jack Northrop's Visionary Aircraft* (Schiffer Military History, Atglen, PA, 1995)

Pape, Garry R. and Campbell, John M. and Donna, *The Flying Wings of Jack Northrop: A Photo Chronicle* (Schiffer Military History, Atglen, PA, 1994)

Rose, Bill, *Secret Projects, Flying Wings and Tailless Aircraft* (Midland/Ian Allan, Hersham, Surrey, 2010)

Simons, Graham M., *Northrop Flying Wings* (Pen & Sword, Barnsley, Yorkshire, 2013)

DOCUMENTS

Baker, Dr Bud, "Clipped Wings, the Death of Jack Northrop's Flying Wing Bombers," *Acquisition Review Quarterly* (Fall 2001)

Flight Operating Instructions, YRB-49A Aircraft, AN 01-15EBB-1 (USAF, September 1950)

Pilot's Handbook for the Model YB-49 Airplane (USAF, 1949)

Pilot's Handbook for the XB-35 Heavy Bombardment Airplane (Report HB-18) (Northrop Aircraft Inc.)

Wooldridge, E. T., *History of the Flying Wing* (www.century-of-flight.net)

INDEX